EMILY

A PLAY

By
STEPHEN METCALFE

SAMUEL FRENCH, INC.
45 WEST 25TH STREET   NEW YORK 10010
7623 SUNSET BOULEVARD HOLLYWOOD 90046
LONDON   TORONTO

Copyright ©, 1989, by Stephen Metcalfe

ALL RIGHTS RESERVED

CAUTION: Professionals and amateurs are hereby warned that EMILY is subject to a royalty. It is fully protected under the copyright laws of the United States of America, the British Commonwealth, including Canada, and all other countries of the Copyright Union. All rights, including professional, amateur, motion pictures, recitation, lecturing, public reading, radio broadcasting, television, and the rights of translation into foreign languages are strictly reserved. In its present form the play is dedicated to the reading public only.

EMILY may be given stage presentation by amateurs in theatres seating less than 500 upon payment of a royalty of Fifty Dollars for the first performance, and Thirty-five Dollars for each additional performance. PLEASE NOTE: for amateur productions in theatres seating over 500, write for special royalty quotation, giving details as to ticket price, number of performances and exact number of seats in your theatre. Royalties are payable one week before the opening performance of the play, to Samuel French, Inc., at 45 W. 25th St., New York, NY 10010; or at 7623 Sunset Blvd., Hollywood, CA 90046, or to Samuel French (Canada), Ltd., 80 Richmond St. East, Toronto, Ontario, Canada M5C 1P1.

Royalty of the required amount must be paid whether the play is presented for charity or gain and whether or not admission is charged.

Stock royalty quoted on application to Samuel French, Inc.

For all other rights than those stipulated above, apply to Wiley Hausam; International Creative Management, Inc., 40 W. 57th St.; New York, NY 10019.

Particular emphasis is laid on the question of amateur or professional readings, permission and terms for which must be secured in writing from Samuel French, Inc.

Copying from this book in whole or in part is strictly forbidden by law, and the right of performance is not transferable.

Whenever the play is produced the following notice must appear on all programs, printing and advertising for the play: "Produced by special arrangement with Samuel French, Inc."

Due authorship credit must be given on all programs, printing and advertising for the play.

Anyone presenting the play shall not commit or authorize any act or omission by which the copyright of the play or the right to copyright same may be impaired.

No changes shall be made in the play for the purpose of your production unless authorized in writing.

The publication of this play does not imply that it is necessarily available for performance by amateurs or professionals. Amateurs and professionals considering a production are strongly advised in their own interests to apply to Samuel French, Inc., for consent before starting rehearsals, advertising, or booking a theatre or hall.

No part of this book may be reproduced, stored in a retrieval system, or transmitted in any form, by any means, including mechanical, electronic, photocopying, recording, or otherwise, without the prior written permission of the publisher.

ISBN 0 573 69087 1   Printed in U.S.A.

IMPORTANT BILLING AND CREDIT REQUIREMENTS

All producers of EMILY *must* give credit to the Author of the Play in all programs distributed in connection with performances of the Play and in all instances in which the title of the Play appears for purposes of advertising, publicizing or otherwise exploiting the Play and/or a production. The name of the Author *must* also appear on a separate line, in which no other name appears, immediately following the title, and *must* appear in size of type not less than fifty percent the size of the title type.

The World Premiere Of

EMILY
By Stephen Metcalfe

Director	Jack O'Brien
Scenic Designer	Douglas W. Schmidt*
Costume Designer	Steven Rubin*
Lighting Designer	David F. Segal
Composer	Bob James
Sound Designer	Michael Holten
Stage Manager	Douglas Pagliotti

Cast of Characters

Emily	Madolyn Smith
Fields	Larry Drake
McCarthy	Steve Rankin
Stein	Jonathan McMurtry*
Hill	William Anton
Hugh	Mitchell Edmonds
Hallie	Margo Martindale
Jon	Kenneth Marshall
Dierdre	Jo deWinter
Mr. Stone	Mitchell Edmonds
Various denizens of Manhattan:	William Anton, Keith Devaney, Jo deWinter, Larry Drake, Susan Gosdick, Jonathan McMurtry*, Margo Martindale, Steve Rankin, Neil Alan Tadken

There will be one fifteen-minute interval.

The time is now.

Assistant Stage Manager: D. Adams

The world premiere of *EMILY* is underwritten in part by generous grants from the following members of the Old Globe Theatre's Director's Council:
De Anza Corporation
National Broadcasting Company
Rams Hill

---

*Associate Artist of the Old Globe Theatre

EMILY was produced in New York City March 29—May 8, 1988, by Manhattan Theatre Club (Lynne Meadow, Artistic Director.) The cast was as follows:

Emily .... LISA BANES
Jason .... JAMES ECKHOUSE
Sean .... DAVE FLOREK
Fields .... JACK KENNY
McCarthy .... DAVE FLOREK
Hill .... ROBERT STANTON
Stein .... JAMES ECKHOUSE
Hugh .... DONALD MAY
Hallie .... HEATHER MAC RAE
Jon .... BRIAN KERWIN
Dierdre .... PATRICIA ENGLUND
Actress/Blanche .... DONNA A. DRAKE
Various Denizens and inhabitants of Manhattan ......
    JAMES ECKHOUSE, PATRICIA ENGLUND,
        DAVE FLOREK, JACK KENNY
      HEATHER MAC RAE, DONALD MAY,
            ROBERT STANTON

Director .... GERALD GUTIERREZ
Set Designer .... HEIDI LANDESMAN
Costume Designer .... ANN HOULD-WARD
Lighting Designer .... PAT COLLINS
Sound Designer .... SCOTT LEHRER
Production Stage Manager ...... DIANNE TRULOCK
Casting .... LYONS/ISAACSON

CAST

EMILY needs a minimum of nine actors. The various supporting characters — the waiters, the restaurant patrons, *et al., are played by the members of the company. The only non-doubling roles are those of John and Emily.*

THE MAJOR CHARACTERS ARE:

Emily Brown

Jason

Sean

Stein

McCarthy

Fields

Hill

Hugh Brown

Hallie

John Stone

Deirdre

The Usher

EMILY

PRODUCTION NOTE: The titles IN CAPS are suggestions. For possible projections. For mood. For setting.

ACT I

NEW YORK AT NIGHT

The couple at a beautifully appointed table seem taken from some modern romantic fairy tale. She is attractive, sparkly-eyed, elegantly dressed without being ostentatious. He is not only incredibly handsome but is a picture of confident, manly, three-piece-suited success. He pours white wine into exquisite crystal wine glasses. In the CANDLELIGHT, the wine glimmers like pale gold. The crystal reflects the gleam of polished tableware. The couple are obviously in love. They stare into one another's eyes, oblivious to the rest of the world. The woman, EMILY BROWN, seems shy, obviously overwhelmed by her own feelings. The man, JASON, raises his glass.

JASON. Hey. To you.
EMILY. Oh, no, please. To you, to you.
JASON. Hey. To us.
EMILY. *(thrilled)* Oh! *(They click glasses and drink. They gaze into each other's eyes.)*

JASON. We are *dangerous.*
EMILY. You think?
JASON. Anything flammable should be kept at a distance. Don't you feel it? *(taking her hand)* Sssss. Hot.
EMILY. *(melting)* Oh! I do feel it, I do, I do. *(JASON chuckles, terribly pleased at his masculine powers.)*
JASON. So. Talk to me. How was your day?
EMILY. *(modestly)* Well...
JASON. Bullish? I bet it was. The market's always up for you. Did you make a million dollars?
EMILY. Almost.
JASON. You're a wonder, Emily.
EMILY. No. A woman.
JASON. *(toasting)* To money. *(They clink and sip and stare into each other's eyes.)*
EMILY. It's so hard to believe we've only known each other a week, Jason. I feel like we've known each other forever.
JASON. I feel the same.
EMILY. Do you? I knew that.

(A ruggedly handsome man passes up and behind the table. EMILY stares.)

JASON. Hello there?
EMILY. *(Pulls her attention back to the table.)* I'm sorry.
JASON. A friend?
EMILY. For a moment I thought he looked familiar but no. *(pause)* Oh, Jason. Do you ever have a hard time telling people the truth? Are you concerned with their feelings?

JASON. Yes, I am.

EMILY. Is it ever difficult for you to tell people how you really feel about them?

JASON. Yes. Yes, it is.

EMILY. Jason ... I shouldn't ask but I've just got to. How do you feel about me? *(The look on JASON'S face says it all. Taking her hand he squeezes it tightly. He growls.)* Yes. Yes, I thought so. *(She reaches into her jacket pocket. She pulls out a velvet jewelry box and places it on the table.)*

JASON. What's that?

EMILY. Darling, I bought this today. *(She opens the box. A diamond ring twinkles in the candlelight.)*

JASON. Oh, my God.

EMILY. Jason, I'm going to be blunt. May I be yours?

JASON. I don't know what to say.

EMILY. Say yes and make me the happiest woman in the world.

JASON. This is awfully sudden.

EMILY. I know.

JASON. This is out of the blue.

EMILY. Sometimes, darling, you have to go with what you feel. *(She turns to a passing waiter.)*

EMILY. May we have a bottle of your finest champagne?

JASON. Emily, for chrissake, we've only known each other a week.

EMILY. Only a week. But a very long week.

JASON. Look, I like you. I do, but...

EMILY. But what?

JASON. What kind of girl wants to marry a guy after

only knowing him a week?

EMILY. Jason, are you saying ... no?

JASON. Emily, I ... I gotta go. *(He quickly rises. He pulls money from his billfold.)*

EMILY. Jason, you can't, I've made all the arrangements!

JASON. Arrangements!?

EMILY. The church, the caterer. I've even been looking at houses in the suburbs.

JASON. Emily, if I wanted a wife and a house in the burbs, I would have stayed in Cincinnati. *(He Exits.)*

EMILY. *(calling after him)* Jason, don't let it end like this! Jason, please! Jason!

(EMILY is paralyzed, her face a mask of shock and disappointment. She bows her head, defeated. The handsome man Enters behind her.)

SEAN. Jesus, Brown, are you proposing marriage again?

EMILY. *(Breaks into a huge, happy grin.)* Hi, Sean!

SEAN. You really are crazy, you know that?

EMILY. Yup.

SEAN. You oughta be seein' a shrink.

EMILY. I love you, Sean. I want you to bear my children.

SEAN. That a proposal?

EMILY. God forbid.

SEAN. When they finished making you, they broke the mold.

EMILY. I know. It's wonderful to be unique.

(The waiter Enters with a bottle of champagne. EMILY takes it and hands it to SEAN.)

EMILY. Champagne?

(EMILY Exits. LIGHT change. EMILY Enters.)

EMILY. *(to the audience:)* Hi. How you doing? Hello. Tsk, okay, what did you think? Back in *the restaurant*. Be honest. A little sneaky? Sort of manipulative? Don't worry, it gets worse. Come on, let's go someplace where we can be alone. *(a self-amused giggle)* Really. I want to tell you all about *me*. I want to tell all about my apartment.

(LIGHT change.)

VAST EMPTY ROOMS!

EMILY. My bedroom! There is nothing in my bedroom but the mattress. The walls are bare. Laundered blouses are stacked on the floor next to the dirty laundry. I keep meaning to get a laundry bag. My living room! The living room is as barren as the bedroom. The only furniture is a chair, a sidetable, a color t.v. with VCR and cable attachment and an exercise bike that I use as a coat rack. I don't keep much in the fridge. A carton of Tropicana, a carton of skim milk, some leftover Chinese, and sometimes but not for long, a carton of Haagen-Dazs! It goes very well with the *Wall Street Journal*. I don't keep anything in the cupboard but instant coffee. I don't wash dishes, I don't clean ovens, when the milk is sour, I drink my coffee black. Pet peeve. Have you ever noticed how the mirror fogs when you're taking your morning shower? Solution. Bring your coffee into the bathroom and dash the dregs onto the mirror. It clears it. What else. I have 23 conservatively cut suits just like this. I can tie my ribbon tie by the feel which is a good thing cause I don't have a bedroom mirror. I have a briefcase. When I head out in the morning I have highheels in my bag and Nike's on my feet. I usually run late. I work on Wall Street. Wall Street! Home of the great business lunch.

(LIGHT change.)

WALL STREET PUB!

(LIGHTS up on a large round table around which FIELDS, McCARTHY, STEIN, HILL, and EMILY are engaged in heated conversations. Everyone talks at once.)

FIELDS. *(to STEIN:)* So I said, look, these stocks are interest sensitive and typically move in the opposite direction of current rates. If you liked it at fifteen, you've got to love it at eleven.

MCCARTHY. *(to HILL:)* Nah, marriage brings joint ownership. In terms of your tax picture, divorce is a great idea. If your wife loves you, she should understand that.

HILL. *(to McCARTHY:)* I can save you up to 90% on that. I am talking size. Real size.

MCCARTHY. Hey, Brown! You want size? *(He grabs his*

crotch.) I'll give you size!

EMILY. McCarthy!?

WAITER. Everything all right, miss?

EMILY. Bite the big one.

WAITER. Very good.

EMILY. *(to the WAITER:)* No, not you.

STEIN. *(to FIELDS:)* We think the Fed will ease up on its growth targets for the coming quarter. They have to. They don't want to be *total* assholes.

EMILY. *(to STEIN:)* Yes, I agree that a world war would be wonderful for your investment portfolio but I think it's a little unrealistic.

STEIN. What about a small skirmish?

EMILY. Are we talking Central America or the Middle East...?

HILL. *(to McCARTHY:)* And so I said, who do you think you're dealing with, Howdy Doody? Huh? Listen to me, I said! I could buy and sell you out of petty cash! *Go* to someone who "appreciates you." Go on! Make my day!

MCCARTHY. Then what?

HILL. Then I told her we'd discuss it when I get home tonight. She knows I don't like her calling me at work.

EMILY. *(to the audience:)* Do you believe this? All we talk is business, business, business. And if it's not business, do you know what it is?

HILL. How 'bout them Mets, huh?

MCCARTHY. Screw the Mets. How about the Yankees?

STEIN. Only six months to the Super Bowl.

FIELDS. Anybody have the number of a good bookie?

STEIN, MCCARTHY and HILL. I do.

EMILY. But mostly we talk about business.

FIELDS. I do not believe the month's projected figures on mutual bonds...

MCCARTHY. Hey, Brown, how about dinner sometime? We'll discuss "mutual bonds."

EMILY. Forget it, McCarthy. From what I hear, your bond's too small for me.

STEIN. It won't solve the company's problem.

HILL. Bet on it. I'd bet on it.

STEIN. They're almost a million in debt.

FIELDS. The new agreement gives them three months to work on restructuring.

MCCARTHY. God, you're a mental midget, Fields.

FIELDS. I'm a graduate of the Harvard Business School.

MCCARTHY. That's what I said.

HILL. What do you think, Brown?

EMILY. I think I would kill for a Hershey bar.

STEIN. A desire for sweets is a sign of sexual frustration.

EMILY. Why is it I get propositioned by someone every two minutes?

ALL THE BOYS. You're a girl.

EMILY. Woman. Do me a favor and proposition each other.

STEIN. Hey, Fields, wanna fuck? *(EMILY glances off left, noticing something.)*

EMILY. Who's that with Montanelli? *(Everyone looks. A moment.)*

STEIN. Her fiance.

MCCARTHY. He's a bondtrader over at Morgan Stanley.

EMILY. *(shocked)* Montanelli's getting married?

MCCARTHY. Incredible, huh? She's smart, she's fun, she puts out, she's one of the nicest girls I know. I don't know why she'd pull a dirty trick like marriage.

HILL. She's in love.

ALL THE BOYS. *(grimacing)* Oooh!

MCCARTHY. Brown, you heard the latest statistics? Something like eight out of ten college-educated career women will not get married!

HILL. We're talking spinsterhood, Brown.

STEIN. We're talking about being basically unfulfilled.

MCCARTHY. We're talking a lifetime of casual affairs.

FIELDS. It's gonna get tougher as you get older, Brown. There's a lot of very splendid, young competition out there.

EMILY. Boys, the reason smart, educated, sensitive women are not getting married is that there are not enough smart, educated sensitive men to go around. I think it's the nature of the beast. And besides, as an emotionally and financially self reliant, individual, why do you think I would ever consider an archaic, self defeating, concrete-booted institution like marriage any kind of fulfillment whatsoever?

ALL THE BOYS. You're a girl.

EMILY. You are all absolutely and totally wrong. *(staring off stage)* Boy, does she look happy. I could kill her.

MCCARTHY. The hell with love. There's nothing less hungry than a blissful broad.
EMILY. *Woman,* McCarthy.
FIELDS. Men do that to girls, make'm blissful.
EMILY. *Women, boys!* We are *women!*
STEIN. She'll end up pregnant.
FIELDS. Cheerful.
HILL. Barefoot and rosy cheeked.
MCCARTHY. Her work will suffer.
STEIN. Cheer up, Brown. Love is a bad career move for a business man.

(They all begin talking at once again, louder and louder. Buzzing like bees, they Exit. EMILY is silent. LIGHT change.)

EMILY. I guess I should take a moment to tell you about my boss. He's a tyrant. He's a maniac. He should squeeze ball bearings. Everyone is terrified of him. He harasses me constantly. He's always calling me into his office for private conferences. He's always asking insinuating, personal questions. It's like he thinks he owns me.

PLUSH, WOOD PANELED OFFICES

(LIGHTS up on a huge desk. The MAN behind the desk is a straight backed and regal as a general. EMILY sits, waiting.)

MAN. *(into the telephone)* America? Don't talk to me about America. I'm talking about business! The average American is more than five thousand dollars in debt and you want to talk to me about America? The average American should know that what's good for Wall Street is good for America, and if he wants it otherwise, he should move to Moscow. You get me some results with those "legislators" or you can say goodbye to Washington D.C. and hello to Juneau, Alaska. *(He slams down the phone. He stares sternly at EMILY. She squirms in her seat. He presses a button on the phone console.)*

HUGH. Hold all calls. *(pause)* You were to be in my office after lunch.

EMILY. It's after lunch.

HUGH. *(rising)* It's three hours after lunch. Stand up, please. *(EMILY does so. He looks like he's going to bite her. Suddenly he breaks into a warm smile. HUGH BROWN, EMILY'S father, holds out his arms.)* Hello, punkin!

EMILY. Hi, Daddy. *(They hug.)*

EMILY. *(to audience:)* Okay, so I kind of gave you the wrong impression. But he's still guilty of harassment.

HUGH. Think fast! Generalized dollar strength.

EMILY. Uh... Above 2.2 West German marks, holding solid at around 7.5 francs and, uh...

HUGH. The yen?

EMILY. The yen, the yen...

HUGH. 166. Of all things you should know about the yen, Emily.

EMILY. Sorry, Daddy.

HUGH. Enough idle chit-chat. To work. Emily, I've put in a bid on a small brokerage firm.

EMILY. How small?

HUGH. Annual gross in the thirty to forty million range.

EMILY. Paltry.

HUGH. Don't be sarcastic. It's a peach of a company, I want it and I will have it. If present management sees no problem in who I put in the driver's seat, there's no reason to believe my takeover will be stalled.

EMILY. Who do you see in the driver's seat, Daddy?

HUGH. You.

EMILY. Daddy ... it's so lonely at the top.

HUGH. Goddammit, Emily!

EMILY. Daddy, your blood pressure.

HUGH. One word and one word only. Commitment!

EMILY. Sorry?

HUGH. To positive action. To coming out on top. To winning. I don't need to remind you that this is all going to be yours some day. Your baby. Your child. A child demands sacrifices. I want to know that you're ready to make that commitment. Punkin, if you wish to consort with eagles, you must grow wings to fly.

EMILY. Daddy? If I consort with eagles will I start wanting worms for breakfast?

HUGH. Emily—

EMILY. And let's say I ran with rats, would I get rabies, Daddy?

HUGH. Stop!

EMILY. If I swim with sharks will I grow gills?

HUGH. Goddammit!

(LIGHT change.)

EMILY. Okay, I guess I sort of drive him crazy too.

HUGH. You're just like your mother, never taking a damn thing seriously!

EMILY. But it's not my fault. Really, it's not. I just get ... sidetracked.

CENTRAL PARK

EMILY. It's a beautiful evening and I'm walking up Central Park West. The park is filled with men. Walking home from work. Jogging. Riding bikes. Shirts off. Nylon shorts soaked with sweat. Sometimes I almost walk right off curbs and blunder into traffic.

(HORNS beep. EMILY jumps back.)

EMILY. I mean ... *(She sees a man.)* What's a girl ... *(and others)* To do? I usually go watch my friend, Hallie, work out.

THE HEALTH CLUB!

(LIGHT change. HALLIE, EMILY'S best friend, is struggling to do a Jane Fonda-like exercise. She grunts with effort. She collapses. HALLIE is a New Yorker by way of Texas.)

EMILY. God, I love weights. I love nautilus equipment. Look around this place. Look at all these girls, Hallie, in their Spandex and Lycra and leg warmers and headbands. Look at them. Sweating. Straining. Lifting. Stretching. Killing themselves. Beating their beautiful bodies into shape.

HALLIE. Sluts. Let me get this straight. You break off the relationship but you want the man to think it's his idea?

EMILY. Yup.

HALLIE. An' so you ask them to marry you, hopin' they'll say no?

EMILY. Knowing they will. It saves their feelings, Hallie. This way they think they're hurting my feelings. And they're not. Nobody's feelings are hurt. Everybody is happy.

HALLIE. I think it's weird. *(rising, looking towards a mirror)* Business lunches are turnin' me into a Pillsbury dough girl. I order salad and end up eatin' a pound a' blue cheese dressing. *(looking around)* I loathe every woman here. Hold my legs while I do some sit ups.

EMILY. I've never been in love, Hallie. Maybe it's because I don't trust love. Love doesn't last. What is love? Love is biology. Love is enzymes. Love is crazy chemicals in the blood stream. Love is secretions. Is an intelligent woman supposed to trust secretions? No.

HALLIE. How many's that?

EMILY. Three. Let's go take a sauna, I'm exhausted.

HALLIE. Emily! I've got to do at least ten!

EMILY. Men are so fragile. I hesitate to get close to a man because I'm afraid I'll hurt him.

HALLIE. Or maybe he'll hurt you.

EMILY. Hallie, please. A woman's heart is as tough as nails.

HALLIE. Right. Ugh! I can't make it.

EMILY. A woman is as tough as nails.

HALLIE. How many's that?

EMILY. Five, let's go take a shower.
HALLIE. Two more.
EMILY. Hearts break. There are harsh words. Tears. Men don't like to cry and so they end up hating you.
HALLIE. Emily, if the right guy came along, you'd kill for him.
EMILY. That's ridiculous.
HALLIE. You wouldn't be able to help yourself.
EMILY. Hallie, a woman can always help herself.
HALLIE. One more. Jesus. Why am I killin' myself like this? The only thing that's losin' weight is my boobs. *(She tries to sit up. She can't.)*
EMILY. Space. A woman needs space.
HALLIE. My stomach wasn't made to sit.
EMILY. A woman needs room to move.
HALLIE. Help me, give me your hand. *(EMILY doesn't. HALLIE collapses.)*
EMILY. A man should give you room.
HALLIE. Men have always given me a lot of room. *(rising)* Gotta run.
EMILY. I thought we were having dinner.
HALLIE. Can't. I! Have got a date!
EMILY. He any good?
HALLIE. He walks, he talks, he breathes. He doesn't make as much money as I do but he's flesh and blood.
EMILY. Is he straight?
HALLIE. Oh, God ... please! *(Exiting)* Talk to you!
EMILY. *(calling after her)* Stay in charge!

(LIGHT change. Behind EMILY, some outdoor cafe tables are being set up.)

EMILY. Okay! It's a balmy summer evening and you're alone. Single. Solo. No plans for the evening. What do you do? You can hit the salad bar at the Korean vegetable market, pick up a movie for the VCR and go home. Or you can stop, sit at a table on the sidewalk and have a drink. Anything can happen.

COLUMBUS AVENUE CAFE!

(LIGHTS up as EMILY sits at a table. Other young, urban professionals have come on to sit at the other tables. A drunken FIELDS, a glass in his hand, Enters.)

FIELDS. Brown! What a coincidence!
EMILY. Fields, what a surprise. I thought I left you at work.
FIELDS. Alone, huh? Guess I better join you.
EMILY. Fields—
FIELDS. You had dinner?
EMILY. Fields—
FIELDS. No problem. You can watch me eat.

(The waiter, JOHN STONE, comes to the table. EMILY, not seeing him, rises.)

EMILY. Fields, I was just leaving.
JOHN. Hi. Can I help you? *(And she looks at him. She stares a moment. She falls back into her chair with a thud.)*
EMILY. White wine, please.
JOHN. Very good. Something for you, sir?
FIELDS. Vodka martini. Straight up. A double. *(JOHN*

turns and walks away. EMILY almost comes to her feet to watch him go. She looks stunned.) Brown, can I give you some personal advice? Not as man to woman but as co-workers. Two people in the same boat. Ready? The way you live your life is crazy. Shall I go on?

EMILY. Please, Fields, you're making my day.

FIELDS. You are preoccupied with the wrong things. You are preoccupied with the opposite sex. It's understandable. You're a female. It's genetic. the opposite sex is not important — I'm talkin' to you like I would to a guy. Money is what's important. Put money in thy purse. William Shakespeare said that. Fill thy purse with money. You have some time?

EMILY. Years.

FIELDS. Let's talk.

(JOHN Enters and puts a martini down in front of FIELDS.)

FIELDS. Sex! *(to JOHN:)* Bring me another right away. *(to EMILY:)* Sex, sex, sex! *(EMILY wants to fall through the floor as JOHN Exits.)* Once upon a time it was all I thought about. I was a mad passionate animal. Believe me, Brown, I was.

EMILY. What changed you, Fields?

FIELDS. I got married. Nothing turns you off on the opposite sex faster than marriage. Brown ... everything I am today I owe to my ex-wife. One word, Brown. Money. Money is stable. Money is giving. You can't count on women at all. No offense but *I* know. I've gone through enough of 'm. But you know where you stand with money. *(FIELDS suddenly reaches and puts his hand on EMILY'S*

hand. EMILY is taken back. Mostly because FIELDS hasn't grabbed her hand but grabbed her wine glass.) Brown?
EMILY. Fields,
FIELDS. I am a happy person.
EMILY. Fields?
FIELDS. Brown?
EMILY. Let go of my wine.
FIELDS. Oh.

(JOHN Enters and puts the martini down in front of FIELDS.)

FIELDS. 'Nother vodka martini. Double.
JOHN. Don't you think you ought to slow down, sir?
FIELDS. Do you know how much money I make a year?
JOHN. Enough to buy the house a drink?
FIELDS. Hah. In a second. *(Sips his martini.)*
JOHN. Drinks for the house! *(FIELDS almost spits out his martini.)*
JOHN. Another for you, miss?
EMILY. I'm fine, really. Thank you. *(JOHN Exits.)*
EMILY. *(Calls after him.)* Thank you very much, really. Thank you!
FIELDS. I guess I told him who's boss.
EMILY. I've got to go, Fields. *(FIELDS desperately grabs EMILY'S briefcase.)*
FIELDS. Brown!
EMILY. Fields!
FIELDS. Men ... are afraid of women like you. Yes. We

are. Don't take it personally. This is equality. Men are afraid of each other. It is a jungle out there. We fight, we envy, we lie. And well we should. Our lives are at stake. All a man can do is try and survive. You, an attractive woman, have chosen to join the battle. You compete with us for bread. When you compete with people, you fear people. We fear each other, Brown. We're terrified of each other. But should we give in to that fear? No. Should we run from it? No. What should we do, Brown? I'll tell you what we should do. We should face the danger head on. We should be brave. Brown? We should sleep together.

EMILY. You're drunk.

FIELDS. Men and women need each other.

EMILY. You just said—

FIELDS. *Forget* what I said! Men and women need each other. They need the tax deductions.

EMILY. Fields—

FIELDS. Okay, don't sleep with me. Marry me! We'll get a station wagon and a golden retriever. We'll live like human beings for chrissake!

EMILY. Fields, don't make me crush your already numbed feelings into chalkdust.

(JOHN Enters and puts the drink down in front of FIELDS.)

FIELDS. You're not a lesbian, are ya? *(Stunned silence. Everyone stares at EMILY. EMILY picks up FIELD'S drink and dumps it over his head. She Exits. FIELDS calls after her.)* Brown! I'll call! We'll talk!

(LIGHT change.)

EMILY. According to Ann Landers, what women really want is a hug. *(pause)* It should be so simple. Sometimes I think what I really want is to figure out what I'm doing with my life. I think about it all the time. Well, not all the time. Most of the time. Actually, not even most of the time. Every now and then. Actually, to be specific, if it's summer and I'm on the Seventh Avenue Express wedged between a bag lady and a ghetto blaster, that's when I wonder what I'm doing with my life. What does this wondering have to do with anything? Despair and futility make you aggressive. I went back to the restaurant where the most beautiful guy I'd ever seen was waiting tables. I figured, what do I got to lose?

(LIGHTS up on the tables. EMILY moves to the one she was at before. She doesn't see JOHN STONE. She is approached by a hostess.)

HOSTESS. Just one?
EMILY. May I sit here?
HOSTESS. Someone will be with you in a moment.

(EMILY sits. She looks around. She doesn't like the seat. She stands and sits in the other. No, the first one had a better view. She stands and immediately bumps into someone behind her. Crash! She turns, startled and is immediately horrified. It is JOHN. He holds a pitcher of water in one hand and a bowl of soup in the other. EMILY has just knocked the bowl of soup down his front. He stands there, frozen in disbelief.)

EMILY. Oh! I'm so sorry!

JOHN. *(trying to control his temper)* It's okay. It was ... my fault. *(She wipes at his shirt and vest and apron with her napkin.)*

EMILY. I wasn't looking and I — oh, I...

JOHN. Really, just—

EMILY. Let me—

JOHN. Really, I'll just go to the back and—

EMILY. I feel horrible, I ... *(EMILY is still trying to clean him. His chest, his stomach, his pants ... She seems quite unaware that she is now wiping at his crotch.)*

JOHN. You don't-have-to-do-that.

EMILY. *(mortified)* Oh!

JOHN. Will your friend be joining you?

EMILY. Oh, you mean the other — He's not my friend. He's ... no one. I'm alone. I'm single. Just me. *(JOHN pours water from his pitcher.)*

JOHN. Our specials this eveing are—

EMILY. Aren't you supposed to say your name is such and such and you'll be my waiter for the evening?

JOHN. My name is John and I—

EMILY. John what?

JOHN. My name is John Stone and I'll be your waiter for the evening.

EMILY. My name is Emily Brown and I'll be your patron for the evening.

JOHN. Our specials this evening, Miss, are—

EMILY. Emily.

JOHN. Emily ... what would you like?

EMILY. Company. *(mesmerized)* Will you have dinner with me?

JOHN. I can't.

EMILY. Why not?

JOHN. I'm working.

EMILY. *(She snaps out of her trance.)* Of course you're working, you're ... you're ... *(again mesmerized)* ... you're beautiful. *(Embarrassed silence. EMILY can think of nothing better to do than pick up her glass of water and drain it. She smiles at JOHN and holds the glass out for a refill. JOHN refills it.)*

JOHN. I'll get you a menu. *(He Exits. EMILY watches him go.)*

EMILY. *(to the audience:)* He seemed magical to me. Like a chivalrous knight of old. With soup on his chest. *(EMILY dumps her water into the plant that is next to her table.)* John Stone!. *(EMILY holds up her empty water glass. She smiles. JOHN Enters, comes over and refills it.)* Thank you! *(He moves away.)* He seemed surrounded by light. He didn't seem to touch the ground when he walked. *(EMILY dumps the water into the plant.)* John Stone!? *(Holds up her empty water glass. She smiles. JOHN Enters, comes to refill it.)* Thank you very much! *(He moves away.)* It's like I could hear voices singing all through dinner.

(The sudden sound of VOICES — they must be angels — singing. EMILY dumps her water into the plant.)

EMILY. John Sto — !

JOHN. *(Places the check in front of her.)* Yes. Check?

EMILY. Could you tell me all about the specials again?

JOHN. Miss...

EMILY. Emily.

JOHN. Emily, what have you got against me? The only way I make any tips is to turn over my tables. You have had a dinner salad, fourteen glasses of water, one glass of white wine, five cups of coffee, you've managed to spread it out over three hours, and in that three hours I've told you our specials twelve times. And! This is what really impresses me. You haven't gone to the bathroom once. Miss...

EMILY. Emily.

JOHN. Emily, what's the story?

EMILY. I've really got to run. *(Hands him the bill and a twenty.)* Keep the change.

JOHN. Even though I deserve it, a twelve dollar tip is too much. Don't go away.

(He strides off. EMILY stands, thinking. She takes her briefcase and shoves it under the table. She moves quickly away. LIGHT change.)

EMILY. Okay, sneaky. I ran home. Have you ever noticed that when you first meet someone you're crazy about, you don't like to admit that you go to the bathroom in front of him? I mean, *I ran.* They stopped serving dinner at 12:30. It was now 9:30. I had just enough time to shower, shampoo, condition and set my hair, do my eyes and figure out what I was going to wear. It's not easy to look perfect, smart, desirable, together, successful and casual all at the same time. *(She glances at her watch, gives a little scream of dismay.)* Time passes quickly when you're having fits of despair. *(She starts off. She comes back.)* I ended up wearing out exactly what I'd worn in.

COLUMBUS AVENUE AT NIGHT

(LIGHTS up on the sidewalk cafe, the tables empty, Waiters are cleaning up, taking the tables inside. EMILY composes herself, and approaches.)

EMILY. John Stone! *(A waiter turns. It's not JOHN STONE.)* Oh. Sorry. Hi, excuse me, is John still here?
WAITER. He left.
EMILY. Oh. Did someone turn in a briefcase?
WAITER. Nope.
EMILY. I left it right — uh ... I *think* I left it right here.
WAITER. No one turned it in. *(He Exits.)*
EMILY. *(sighing)* Thanks.

DARK CITY STREETS!

(The tables are cleared. EMILY is alone. She stands a moment, discouraged.)

EMILY. You're probably worried about me walking home alone. You're sweet. Don't worry, I'm perfectly safe. Okay, it is late. I am a strikingly attractive woman. Unescorted. Unprotected. This *is* New York City. Dark alleyways. Iron bars on apartment windows. Central Park is filled with muggers, rapists and white slavers. But really, I've lived here my whole life. I can take care of myself.

(She doesn't see JOHN Enter behind her. He is in running shoes,

nylon shorts, t-shirt.)

JOHN. Hey. *(She shrieks in fright and turns.)*
JOHN. What?
EMILY. You startled me.
JOHN. *(He holds out her briefcase.)* Sorry. You forgot this. I didn't want to leave it around the bar, things get lost. I was going to run by your place.
EMILY. You don't know my address.
JOHN. I went through your little black book. I figured your kind of address had a doorman. *(pause)* You want this or not? I mean, I'll keep it.
EMILY. *(taking it)* No! Thank you ... How come you're, you know ... going to a track meet?
JOHN. I run at night after work. I'm training for the marathon.
EMILY. Oh, well, what a coincidence.
JOHN. You run?
EMILY. Oh, yes, I do about several hundred miles a week. I mean, not all at once. And I don't do them fast. Slow and steady wins the race, that's my motto.
JOHN. You're not a runner, are you?
EMILY. No. But maybe after you run we could get a drink or something. A milkshake, ten or twelve beers, a blood transfusion.
JOHN. New York women sure are forward.
EMILY. No, we're not. Do you have a girlfriend? I mean, are you involved? Married?
JOHN. Do you always blurt out personal questions at people you hardly know?
EMILY. Yes, but give me time and you'll find I compen-

sate for it by constantly blurting out personal information. Okay, what are you, an actor, musician or writer?

JOHN. Why would I be any of those things?

EMILY. You're a waiter. And every waiter in this town is an—

JOHN and EMILY. *(together)* —actor, musician or writer.

JOHN. Yah. Actor. Aspiring. So when do I learn something about you?

EMILY. I'm a stockbroker. But I see a lot of Broadway shows.

JOHN. I haven't seen one. Can't afford it. Well ... gotta go. I have eight miles to do. *(Pause. He smiles. She smiles.)*

EMILY. What?

JOHN. You want to get together some time?

EMILY. I hardly know you. When?

JOHN. I'll call you. *(He heads off.)*

EMILY. Let me give you my card!

JOHN. I don't need your card. I went through your book.

EMILY. All my friends say I'm a nice person!

JOHN. *(Exiting.)* No kidding?

EMILY. Hey! Are we really gonna get together? I mean, don't do me any favors! If you think playing hard to get is going to work with this kid you're ... *(to the audience:)* absolutely right.

JOHN. *(off)* Emily? I'll call!

(LIGHT change.)

EMILY. Well ... he didn't. At least not right away. Men don't. And another thing about men. When they do call, they call at the worst possible times. Like during a red alert!

WALL STREET OFFICES!

(Chaos as desks slide on behind EMILY. LIGHTS up on STEIN, McCARTHY, HILL and FIELDS. They are all talking at once, buzzing into phones, hanging up phones, answering phones. EMILY moves to her desk where she sits and stares contentedly into space.)

FIELDS. THE DOW IS FALLING! THE DOW IS FALLING!
HILL. Churning the account? This man would trample his grandmother for an eighth!
MCCARTHY. *(aside)* Call 911. I got a jumper on my hands!
STEIN. I have got paper on my desk beyond your wildest dreams. Trust me!
FIELDS. If this is true, Kemosabe, we are talking blood in the streets!

(HUGH BROWN has Entered. He starts towards EMILY who is still doing nothing.)

STEIN. Battle stations, Emily, battle stations. This is not a drill, repeat, this is not—
HUGH. Carry on, Mr. Stein. Carry on, Emily. Pretend I'm not here. Perhaps you'd like a pad and some charcoal pencils. You could do some doodling.

(EMILY'S PHONE rings. EMILY grabs for it.)

EMILY. Emily Brown!

(JOHN's voice is AMPLIFIED through speakers.)

JOHN. Hi, this is John Stone.
EMILY. Who? — Hi! *(catching herself—turning businesslike)* Hello, yes, how are things in Tokyo?
JOHN. What? Oh. Can't talk, huh?
EMILY. That's affirmative.
JOHN. Sorry I didn't call right away. I've been busy. I've been taking some extra shifts.
EMILY. I would say that's a fine investment strategy with excellent potential.
JOHN. Still want to grab that milkshake?
EMILY. I think a face to face would be rewarding.
JOHN. I have a class. After that?
EMILY. Fine. I'll look forward to it. *(She hangs up. She smiles innocently at her father.)*
HUGH. Got a live one, huh?
EMILY. Mmm-hmm.
HUGH. I like your style. A little distant. A little hard to get. A good broker should always make them come to him. *(All the eavesdropping brokers slam their phones down as one.)*
HUGH. Keep up the good work, Emily.
EMILY. I'll try.

(PHONES start ringing. The brokers leap to answer them. EMILY'S PHONE rings.)

EMILY. Emily Brown.
JOHN. *(again, over speakers)* I thought you might like a time and place.
EMILY. Love it.

(LIGHT change. The desks slide off.)

RIVERSIDE PARK!

EMILY. The thing I love about being with someone you hardly know is you can ask them anything cause you don't know the answer.

(JOHN Enters. He carries two cans of soda. He hands one to EMILY.)

JOHN. There we go. One cold can of pop.
EMILY. So how long have you been in New York?
JOHN. How do you know I'm not a New Yorker?
EMILY. Because no real New Yorker would be caught dead calling diet soda, pop.
JOHN. How do you know that?
EMILY. I know. I grew up here. Private girl's school. Barnard College.
JOHN. I've been here about two months.
EMILY. Any more like you on the farm? Any brothers? I have friends who'd be interested.
JOHN. No brothers. Five sisters.
EMILY. I'm sure you're totally screwed up because of it.
JOHN. *(a small smile)* Maybe only a little bit.

EMILY. Where you from?

JOHN. Minnesota.

EMILY. Isn't that near the Arctic Circle? Don't Eskimos and Swedes and strange ethnic types like Mary Tyler Moore live there?

JOHN. Yup.

EMILY. Where'd you go to school?

JOHN. You preppies always want to know where somebody went to school.

EMILY. I'm not a—

JOHN. Minnesota. University of. The Golden Gophers.

EMILY. God. You're normal. Being with you is like eating health food. Your parents can't be divorced.

JOHN. My parents are crazy about each other.

EMILY. That's very unusual.

JOHN. Yeah, I guess it is.

EMILY. *(sadly)* My parents were divorced when I was three years old. *(brightening)* There. Personal information blurted out.

JOHN. Why do I get the feeling it's a little well rehearsed?

EMILY. What a mean thing to say!

JOHN. What do you want me to say?

EMILY. Most men say something sympathetic and sweet.

JOHN. So it is well rehearsed.

EMILY. Well, yeah, but just because something's well practiced, doesn't make it less true. How about I take you out to dinner?

JOHN. What about that milkshake?

EMILY. It's after seven o'clock. It's illegal to drink a milkshake in this town after seven o'clock. Not to mention what it does to your reputation. *(pause)* Come on. I'll take you to my favorite place. Come on.

(JOHN moves away. LIGHT change.)

EMILY. You might have the feeling I was getting off on the wrong foot by stepping all over his. Well, don't worry, like I said, it gets worse.

TAVERN ON THE GREEN AT NIGHT

EMILY. My favorite restaurant is dark, romantic, elegant and filled with candlelight. John, looking gorgeous in polo shirt and jeans, is slightly underdressed. This, I assume, is what seems to have him on edge.

(LIGHTS up on a table. EMILY moves to join JOHN. A WAITER approaches with menus as they sit.)

WAITER. Bon soir!
EMILY. Bon soir, Jean-Claude!
WAITER. For mademoiselle.
EMILY. Merci.
WAITER. For monsieur. *(He hands JOHN a clip-on tie as well as a menu. JOHN sheepishly puts it on. The WAITER Exits.)*
EMILY. Isn't this nice? *(JOHN opens the menu. He closes their menu.)*

EMILY. Know what you want already?

JOHN. I cannot afford this place. The entrëes are more than my rent.

EMILY. Don't worry, it's on me.

JOHN. It is *not* ... on you.

EMILY. Of course it's not. It's on my expense account. Don't you know you're a potential client?

JOHN. I am *not* a potential client.

EMILY. Are you interested in stocks and bonds? Yes, Emily, I'm interested in stocks and bonds. Shall we discuss it over dinner? I'd love to, Emily. You're a potential client.

JOHN. You pull this scam often?

EMILY. Scam. *(trying to control her temper)* If you must know, my company expects me to do this.

JOHN. Really.

EMILY. Yes, really. They need the tax write-offs.

JOHN. If people who could afford to pay their taxes, did, then people who can't afford to, wouldn't have to.

EMILY. I pay taxes, buster, believe me, I do. You know what my taxes subsidize? The National Endowment for the Arts! What's the matter with you, huh? Why do you have to be such a ... a male!

JOHN. Why are you trying to take total control of the evening?

EMILY. I don't do that! I never do that! *(to the audience:)* I always do that. *(to JOHN:)* When somebody wants to do something nice for you, why can't you accept it gracefully?

JOHN. Maybe I could accept it gracefully if you could

offer it gracefully.
EMILY. I am renowned for my social grace.
JOHN. Or your lack of it.
EMILY. Drop dead! *(He stares at her. He rises. He drops the clip-on tie in front of her. He leaves. Silence.)* Well, I guess I told him. Men are so fragile. I hesitate to get close to a man because I'm afraid I'll hurt him. I hate it when feelings get hurt. *(fighting tears)* I just hate it. *(She rises and leaves the table.)*

MIDTOWN CROSS STREETS.

(LIGHT change. JOHN Enters. She doesn't see him at first. She looks up. They stare at one another. He crosses to her.)

JOHN. I apologize.
EMILY. No, I do.
JOHN. You were right.
EMILY. No, you were.
JOHN. We could compromise.
EMILY. I'm very good at compromise. If we do what I want, I'll shut up. *(He smiles, gently caresses her hair.)*
EMILY. We'll do what you want if you do that again.
JOHN. We could do simple things.
EMILY. In New York City?
JOHN. You still hungry?
EMILY. Always.
JOHN. Come on.

(LIGHT change. A hot dog VENDOR has Entered. EMILY and JOHN approach him.)

JOHN. How many pups?

EMILY. Pups?

JOHN. Hot dogs, baby!

EMILY. They're probably loaded with carcinogens and nitrates and, I dunno, rat's feet.

JOHN. How many?

EMILY. Three.

JOHN. *(to the VENDOR:)* Six pups with everything. And — what the heck, you only live once, we'll splurge — two *large* papayas.

EMILY. I feel like I fell asleep and woke up on the Good Ship Lollipop. Three pups and a large papaya seem so G-rated.

VENDOR. Four seventy.

EMILY. I got it. *(JOHN stops her.)* Oh, come on. You wait tables. I make more than I know what to do with.

JOHN. Maybe I'm old fashioned but—

EMILY. You're medieval.

JOHN. But when I ask a girl out, I like to pay her way.

EMILY. You're medieval but nice.

VENDOR. Somebody gonna pay for this a what?

JOHN. Four seventy.

EMILY. I got the tip.

(She winces at the look he gives her. LIGHT change. The VENDOR Exits.)

EMILY. *(to the audience:)* I had this feeling someone was going to throw me off Wall Street for failure to contribute conspicuously to the economy. We ate pups. We walked. We talked. you know what? Well, you'll see...

CENTRAL PARK WEST AT NIGHT

(LIGHTS on EMILY and JOHN.)

JOHN. So anyway, after grad school I spent six years at the Guthrie as part of the company. Finally I decided it was time to give New York a shot. So here I am. Waiting tables.

EMILY. Here I am. Home.

JOHN. Anyway. I guess maybe I am a little sensitive about it. This living hand to mouth seems like such a cliche. What I'm trying to say is ... I appreciate you wanting to buy me dinner.

EMILY. And next time you'll let me.

JOHN. Maybe. *(pause)*

EMILY. Boy, I hate this moment. Waiting for a guy to kiss you for the first time.

JOHN. Guess we better get it over with. *(A moment. They start to kiss. Closer ... almost ... and then:)* I feel like a jerk.

EMILY. No, your instincts are great, really.

JOHN. You ever wonder what we're doing?

EMILY. Kissing?//
JOHN. Dating.
EMILY. Oh, is that what we're doing?
JOHN. You ever find yourself noticing couples? I do. You know what I like? I like the way a woman holds a man's arm as they walk. The way a man sort of rests his fingers on the back of a woman's neck as they stare in store windows. The way they talk. Or when they don't, the way the silence doesn't beg to be filled. I like that. *(a moment)* Pay no attention to me. I meet somebody I like, I make up a sotry and assign them a part all in the first two minutes.
EMILY. What if they can't play it?
JOHN. I get disappointed. *(And suddenly, without warning, he kisses her. A long, lovely kiss.)* I'll walk you up.
EMILY. *(quickly)* That's okay. Will you call me? Better yet, why don't I call you?
JOHN. I don't have a phone.
EMILY. What? How are you going to get obscene phone calls if you don't have a phone?
JOHN. Got a pen? A piece of paper?
EMILY. *(looking in her bag)* I have a pen. *(JOHN writes on her hand.)*
JOHN. I share this place with three other guys. We figured if we didn't get a phone, nobody would get stuck for the bill.
EMILY. What's this?

JOHN. My service. *(He kisses her, again taking her by surprise. The kiss leaves her dizzy and just about reeling.)* Bye. *(He turns and walks. EMILY seems paralyzed.)*
EMILY. John! I had such a nice time. *(He smiles. He turns and Exits. To audience: A happy sigh.)* Well...

(LIGHT Change.)

EMILY. Enough about all of you. Let's talk about *me* for awhile. Picture this if you will. A luxury apartment building on the Upper East Side. I jump out of a taxi cab — I'm late as usual. I'm bearing gifts. One gift to be precise, wrapped in Tinkerbell ribbons and ducky paper. The apartment is large and luxurious. It is filled with women. Just women. All women. The guest of honor is opening packages. A birthday party, you say? No. I am at the bizzaro world version of a bachelor party.

BABIES!

(HALLIE and DEIRDRE and the rest of the company Enter. The company, men and women alike, are silhouetted upstage. There is the sudden sound of women laughing and chatting.)

HALLIE. I just love baby showers.
DEIRDRE. Please.
EMILY. Hi, everybody!

THE COMPANY. *(in high pitched voices)* Hi!

DEIRDRE. Well, look who's finally here.

EMILY. *(to HALLIE and DEIRDRE:)* Sorry I'm late.

DEIRDRE. Lucky you're late. *(EMILY kisses DEIRDRE'S cheek.)*

EMILY. Hello, Mother.

HALLIE. Emily, you almost missed everything. I didn't think you were goin' to make it.

DEIRDRE. I thought you were smarter than this.

HALLIE. Pregnancy is so beautiful.

DEIRDRE. Thank god it isn't contagious. *(The company breaks into a high pitched gush — Awwww!*

DEIRDRE. Dear God, what has she opened now?

HALLIE. *(thrilled)* Booties!

DEIRDRE. Emily, I think you're going to need a bloody to survive this.

HALLIE. They're so cutie-bootie-whootie!

DEIRDRE. I know I am.

EMILY. Mother. *(The company breaks into another high pitched gush — Awwww! DEIRDRE winces.)*

DEIRDRE. How's the bastard, dear?

EMILY. He's buying a company.

DEIRDRE. He's in ecstasy then. Flexing his wallet always brings out the savage in him.

EMILY. He wants me to run it.

DEIRDRE. Do it, darling. Run it right into the ground for me.

EMILY. I wish you and Daddy could be civil to one another.

DEIRDRE. I adore your father, dear. I really do. I've just found that the best way to get his attention is to make his life as miserable as possible.

EMILY. It isn't that way at all and you know it.

HALLIE. Still seein' the new guy?

DEIRDRE. What's this?

HALLIE. Emily has a new guy.

DEIRDRE. You do? And you haven't said a word about him to me?

HALLIE. They went out. He walked her home. He asked if he could come up.

EMILY. Hallie, if I want my mother to know all about my personal life, I can tell her myself.

DEIRDRE. So tell me, darling. Details, I want details.

HALLIE. She doesn't have any yet. She said no.

DEIRDRE. Why did you say no, darling? Was he an undesirable boogieman?

HALLIE. She wanted him so much she was weak in the knees.

EMILY. Hallie!

DEIRDRE. Why didn't you invite him up then?

EMILY. Mother!

HALLIE. She was scared.

EMILY. Wrong.

HALLIE. She was nervous.

EMILY. I was not!

DEIRDRE. What were you, darling?

EMILY. I... I don't know what I was. Mother, I've never had a man in my apartment for the night.

DEIRDRE. Oh, how dreary.

HALLIE. She always wants the option of bein' able to leave quickly in the morning.

EMILY. Let's put it this way. If your home is a reflection

of you, than me is a mess. *(The company gushes on cue — Awwww!)*

HALLIE. She's opening mine! That's mine! That's from me! *(The company gushes again.)* A cuddly bear! *(HALLIE is so joyful, she's on the verge of tears.)* I liked it so much, I bought one for me. *(pause; sadly)* My biological clock feels like it's tickin' away on a musty old shelf in the attic.

DEIRDRE. If I hear one more speech about a woman's fleeting childbearing years, I'll be sick.

HALLIE. I want children. What's wrong with children?

DEIRDRE. For one thing you can't take them to restaurants without them screaming.

EMILY. Mother, you had children. If I'm not mistaken, you had me.

DEIRDRE. Yes, and all I can say is thank god for boarding schools. I was never meant to be a mother and I knew it. Your father insisted.

HALLIE. I want perspective in my life. I want to make something other than money. I do want to be a mother.

DEIRDRE. Then be one.

HALLIE. It takes two to tango, Deirdre.

DEIRDRE. And you never get asked to dance?

HALLIE. Not permanent.

DEIRDRE. Darlings, listen to me because I am wise and I know these things. You want something that does not exist. You want to be Blondie to some Dagwood with the house and the neighbors and the son and daughter and the dog named Daisy under the kitchen table and if you have that, you'll be happy. You won't. You want fulfillment? Go shopping.

HALLIE. Deirdre, who do you turn to when you're old?
(DEIRDRE is silent.)
EMILY. Reality rears its ugly head.
DEIRDRE. This man you're so terrified of, darling, are you seeing him again?
EMILY. Yes. We're doing cheap, simple, inexpensive things.
THE COMPANY, HALLIE and DEIRDRE. *(aghast)* In New York?
EMILY. They're there if you look for them.

(LIGHT change. JOHN Enters.)

EMILY. *(to the audience:)* I'd call his service. He'd call me at work and miss me. I'd call his service again. He'd call me at home and miss me. *(to the Exiting company:)* No wonder actors are unemployed. You can never find one when you need one! *(to the audience:)* Anyway, finally contact was made. We made plans. We decided to go everywhere! On the subway. We went to the Metropolitan Museum.

THE MET!

(JOHN takes EMILY in his arms and they kiss passionately.)

EMILY. *(to the audience:)* We looked at the art. We went on the Circle Line Ferry.

THE GEORGE WASHINGTON BRIDGE

(JOHN kisses her again.)

EMILY. It's a very nice view of the George Washington Bridge. We went and had a very nice picnic in the Cloisters.

THE CLOISTERS

(JOHN kisses her.)

EMILY. *(breathless)* It was a religious experience. We even went to the Bronx Zoo. *(They kiss.)* And looked at the monkeys.

MONKEYS!

(They kiss passionately. LIGHT change.)

CENTRAL PARK WEST AT NIGHT

JOHN. Invite me up.
EMILY. Let's go over to your place.
JOHN. I have three roomates, one bedroom.
EMILY. We'll lock ourselves in the bathroom.
JOHN. Emily, why won't you invite me up?
EMILY. My ... the place is a mess.
JOHN. I'm not coming up for a tour of your apartment.
EMILY. John, you can't, really, you just — I'm invited to a party tomorrow night. You want to come? *(to audience:)* I'd been telling all my friends about him. They wanted to meet him.

PARTY PEOPLE!

(LIGHT change. A blast of raucous laughter. MUSIC. Well dressed people Enter and surround EMILY and JOHN. They hand them drinks. They mill about, drinking and chatting. EMILY, HALLIE, JOHN, McCARTHY, FIELDS, HILL and STEIN are all standing in a buzzing group.)

FIELDS. So! You wait tables. How incredibly demeaning.
HALLIE. He's not a waiter. He's an actor.
JOHN. Aspiring.
HALLIE. I love actors almost as much as cowboys. Maybe more. Actors take off their hats before they go to bed with you.
HILL. I waited tables once. Summer between my junior and senior year in college. On Nantucket. What a time. Immense amounts of brewski and the drugs were righteous.
FIELDS. Let's have a drink!
EMILY. *(to the audience:)* Everything was going quite well. Really!
STEIN. Afraid I missed the last elections. I was tarpon fishing in the Keys.
FIELDS. We like this little girl. Let me tell you something. Not only is she built, she's smart. Freshen that for you?
MCCARTHY. I'm into ocean sailboat racing myself. Five day babies. The real thing. Choices. Like do we tack today or do we do it under the full moon at 5:30 tomorrow.

EMILY. *(to the audience:)* I could tell John was having a wonderful time.

HALLIE. Where'd you go to school, John?

JOHN. *(looking at EMILY)* Minnesota.

FIELDS. *(raising his hand)* Harvard! *(All cheer.)*

MCCARTHY. *(raising his hand)* Yale! *(All cheer.)*

HILL. Dartmouth! *(All cheer.)*

STEIN. Amherst. *(All are silent.)*

EMILY. I was very pleased that John fit in so well with my friends.

STEIN. Art! I love it! It's such a gossamer thing. Sort of like ... the dollar.

FIELDS. Come on! Let's roll back the furniture, get naked and boogie!

ALL. Fields.

HALLIE. How do you feel about single motherhood? Don't you think there comes a time when a women should just take her fate into her own hands?

EMILY. Everyone went out of their way to be nice to him.

HALLIE. Do you think Emily would mind if we slept together? There'd be no commitments. I'm just interested in your essence.

EMILY. John was very interested in what we all did for a living.

HILL. Have you ever considered the idea that U.S. foreign policy is dedicated to nothing more than preserving big business's gluttonous consumption of the earth's natural resources? Think about it.

JOHN. I have. Have you ever considered that big business is screwing the world completely?

HILL. Yeah. It's great!

EMILY. And I guess the wonderful thing was that we all had more in common then we knew.

ALL. Art!

HILL. Eraserhead!

STEIN. I saw it on a double bill with Pink Flamingos.

MCCARTHY. Ooh, ooh, Cage Flesh! Have you seen that one?

HALLIE. How about Repo Man!?

STEIN. Anything by Woody Allen!

HALLIE. Clint Eastwood!

FIELDS. Hey, hey! You know who I really love? Richard Pryor!

HILL. Especially when he does his impression of white guys!

MCCARTHY. Okay, back off, peckerhead!

HALLIE. I die!

FIELDS. Hey! Hey! Let's all go out for some sushi! *(Everyone Exits, talking excitedly. There is a last blast of raucous laughter and then silence. JOHN and Emily stand there.)*

EMILY. Walking home after, it seemed to me that John, all in all, had had a wonderful time.

(LIGHT change.)

CENTRAL PARK WEST AT NIGHT

EMILY. It was terrible, wasn't it.

JOHN. No.

EMILY. You were uncomfortable, I could tell.

JOHN. No.

EMILY. My friends are dorks.

JOHN. At least they're successful dorks.

EMILY. All they talk about are their jobs, the money they make at their jobs and how they're going to spend their money on vacations away from their jobs.

JOHN. My friends are no different from yours, you know. Except we don't talk about jobs, we talk about parts. The parts we didn't get, the parts we hope we'll get and the parts somebody else always seems to get. We don't talk about money because none of us makes any.

EMILY. John, I think it's wonderful what you're doing.

JOHN. I'm glad one of us does. Tonight's one of those nights where I feel like I'm kidding myself. Jesus, what you are in this town might as well be your name. Hi, how are you? I'm waiter. I mean, what *am* I doing, Emily? Why am I living like this? I'm accomplishing nothing. I have nothing.

EMILY. You have me. *(aghast)* I don't believe I just said something that incredibly stupid. *(JOHN sadly stares at her.)* What?

JOHN. When they made you, they broke the mold, Emily.

EMILY. So I've heard.

JOHN. Thanks for the party, okay? *(He starts to leave.)*

EMILY. John? John, wait. *(He stops.)* Aren't you going to ask if you can come up?

JOHN. See you, Emily.

EMILY. John. *(He stops.)* Do you want to come up?

(silence) I want you to. *(silence)* Come up.

VAST EMPTY ROOMS

(LIGHT change. JOHN looks around in sudden surprise. EMILY stands there embarrassed.)

EMILY. I ... I haven't quite gotten around to fixing it up yet.
JOHN. How long you been here?
EMILY. About ... four.
JOHN. Weeks? Months?
EMILY. Years. *(silence)*
EMILY. I could open a bottle of wine?
JOHN. I'm fine. *(pause)* Well, it's ... roomy. *(And "roomy" seems to echo through the empty space.)*
EMILY. It's a big empty joke. *(She turns and walks away. She feels like she wants to cry.)*
JOHN. Is this why you didn't want to invite me up?
EMILY. I feel so dumb.
JOHN. You're not dumb. *(He kisses her.)* You're great. Have any candles?

(LIGHT change.)

CANDLES

EMILY. Okay, look, so I've slept with a lot of guys. What's a lot? Things just happen. I mean, you're at a party and you meet somebody and they're cute and kind of nice and I mean, he's head-to-toe Paul Stuart and a lawyer or something and he says he has every tape out out by Windham Hill, and so I mean, really, you feel like you can trust him. I know, people are supposed to get to know each other better. But most of the people I know, myself included, have spent all this time cultivating great first impressions and once we get to know each other better, we just don't like each other half as much. So there he is, right then and now, paying attention. And when they clear the furniture and the Stones come on, he's not a bad dancer. What can I say? All of a sudden you're sharing a cab uptown and he invites you up for some Stoli and Truscuits and so, okay, sure, and you're sitting on the couch and he kisses you and it's nice and it's kind of late to go on home now and by coming up you've sort of said yes already, right? And so you do 'cause, I mean, things just happen. And it's not that it's bad. And god knows, you're careful. These days you have to be. No, it's just that ... sometimes you feel like you've done something wrong. You feel like it's supposed to mean more. Well, you get over that. Or used to it. Sort of. I mean, I'm always getting all mindless about sex, especially during the dry spells when I'm convinced that I'm never going to sleep with anyone ever again. But then I do. And what I don't understand is that sometimes right in the middle of it, I find myself thinking — ooh, this is so much more fun to be obsessed with at a distance. It's nicer fantasizing about, right? Yeah, well, let me tell you something. When you're just crazy about someone and you feel it in your bones that they're crazy about you, making love is ... it's more than it's cracked up to be. It's every cliche you've ever heard of. Time *does* stop. And that's what that night was like. He was romantic and tender and strong. And he shared equal time on the bottom. And he made the neatest little sounds deep in his throat. You didn't want it to end. It scared me shitless. Too much of it and you'd be turned off on meaningless sex for good. When I woke up the next morning, John wasn't there. He'd gone out.

(EMILY yawns. LIGHT change. JOHN Enters, a bag of groceries in his arms.)

JOHN. Hey, you're up. I went out to get some stuff for breakfast.

EMILY. What'ja get?

JOHN. Not much. Just some juice-milk-eggs-bacon-bread-jelly-butter-napkins. Some real coffee. I cleaned up your kitchen. Jesus, Emily, you had stuff growing in your refrigerator. Hey, you know what we ought to do with all this money you make? Buy you some furniture. This will shock you, but some people actually own things. Tables, couches, rugs, chairs. Plants. *(Exiting)* I'll help you pick'm out.

EMILY. *(to audience:)* I don't know why, but suddenly I felt nervous.

JOHN. *(coming back)* Some people own more than one towel too. *(Exiting)* You like your eggs scrambled?

EMILY. Very — nervous.

(LIGHT change.)

EMILY. Nerves quickly gave way to confusion, confusion soon led to anxiety, anxiety then threw me up into the toilet bowl of emotional turmoil. Confused, anxiety ridden, and emotionally torn, I did what any red-blooded, all-American girl would do. *(in a little girl voice)* I went to my Daddy. *(normally)* I forgot one thing. Daddy was not Ward Cleaver or Robert Young. Daddy was Goldfinger.

WALL STREET OFFICES

(HUGH Enters. He is going through a folder of papers.)

Emily. What am I afraid of, Daddy?!
Hugh. Not now, Emily.
Emily. What's the matter with me?
Hugh. I can answer that. You don't take your work seriously.
Emily. Daddy, for once in your life be warm and wonderful.
Hugh. Good god, Emily, I'm a businessman!
Emily. Half of me feels like Hallie but half of me feels like Mother.
Hugh. Don't bring up your mother. I'm in a good mood.
Emily. Daddy, he has me buying things.
Hugh. Good god! Are you involved with some gigolo?
Emily. Not for him! For me! I've been buying things for me! I bought a carpet Sunday. I now have a carpet. This carpet goes beautifully with the new couch and the new coffee table and the plants.
Hugh. *(frowning with distaste)* Plants?
Emily. There are green things growing in my living

room, Daddy! Green things begging to be watered!

HUGH. Never much liked plants. They die and rot. But other than plants, I don't understand what the hell's wrong with having a few nice things in your apartment.

EMILY. Wrong? Wrong!? I'll tell you what's wrong! I feel obligated to them. I fell responsible for them. They demand a maturity I don't think I possess because, Daddy, I don't like feeling obligated to or responsible for anything!

HUGH. *(coolly)* I trust you'll soon get over that. *(a moment)* Emily, if this young man is a problem, dump him. Find another one. There are too many fish in the sea.

(HUGH Exits. LIGHT change.)

EMILY. He's right. There are so many men in the world. They're everywhere. I dream sometimes that I know each and every one of them personally. They all smile at me and wave at me. I can see them as they all go down on one knee in front of me and offer me their hearts. In my dreams, I modestly accepts their accolades. Businessmen, farmers, construction workers, cowboys on horses, sword-bearing musketeers, matadors in suits of lights, knights of the round table. They all blow kisses. They all throw flowers. They follow me as I walk through Central Park, pleading, beseeching, begging for my favor. They surround me. They lift me up high, cheering. I beam, radiant beyond measure. But then, in my dreams, I see ... one man, one special man, by himself, beckoning for me. He beckons again. Surrounded by men, I don't know what to do. The one man sadly turns and walks away. I watch him go. And suddenly in my dream, I'm alone. No men. No man. Me. And I feel ... *(joyously)* RELIEVED! Yes. When you're alone, there is no one who can hurt you. Or disappoint you. Or expect anything of you. *(She holds up the velvet jewelry box. She opens it and the diamond ring catches the light.)* Especially that. Expect anything of you.

IMPATIENT PEOPLE

(LIGHT change. People impatiently cluster, either waiting to be seated at tables or trying to get to the bar. JOHN hurries past as EMILY Enters.)

EMILY. John...?
JOHN. Emily! Hey! We're running totally crazy here. See if you can grab a drink at the bar and I'll—
EMILY. John, I have to talk to you. I have to ask you something.
PATRON. Waiter, how much longer for a table!?
JOHN. Can you do it quick?
EMILY. John.
JOHN. Yeah.
PATRON 2. Can we at least order a drink while we're waiting!?
EMILY. John.
PATRON 1. We *had* a reservation!
JOHN. The hostess will be with you in a minute. Jesus, Emily, I have tables.

EMILY. John, is it ever difficult for you to tell people how you feel about them?
JOHN. Huh? I guess. Sometimes.

(Another WAITER rushes through.)

WAITER. John, I accidentally just dumped a bowl of steamed mussels all over your table five!
JOHN. Oh, god.
EMILY. John! And how do you feel about me?
JOHN. Is that the something important you wanted to ask me?
EMILY. No.
PATRON 1. Waiter, we've been waiting forever!
PATRON 3. Waiter, we have to make an 8:00 curtain!
JOHN. Somebody'll be right there!
EMILY. John, what I wanted to say is...
PATRON 2. I want to see the manager!
EMILY. I bought something today.
JOHN. What?
WAITER. John, your table two is screaming for a check and I'm losing my mind!
JOHN. Emily, I have tables, what!?
EMILY. Oh, please. This! *(She holds up the velvet case. Sudden silence. JOHN stares at the ring.)*
JOHN. Are you asking me to marry you? *(And now, with the moment upon her, EMILY hesitates. But then:)*
EMILY. What's the use, I'm hopeless. *(signing the death warrant.)* John, will you marry me?
JOHN. Yes.
EMILY. What? *(He takes the ring out of the velvet box. He*

holds it out to her.)

JOHN. Emily, will you marry me?

EMILY. You're kidding. He's kidding. Are you kidding? He's not kidding?

(He slips the ring on her finger and kisses her. The patrons all applaud. LIGHTS to black. The last thing seen is EMILY'S shocked, stunned face as she turns her head towards the audience.)

END OF ACT I

ACT II

LIGHTS up on EMILY.

EMILY. Let's try to put this mess into perspective and see if it makes any sense. Here's how it works. John and I have this relationship. The commitments inherent in the relationship frighten me. I want out of the commitments but I don't want out of the relationship and so I make a proposal for a relationship that demands even greater commitment, thinking that greater commitment will make him want the relative security of noncommitment but not necessarily the relative emotional desert of a non-relationship. He tricks me. He opts for commitment *and* relationship and somehow gets me to accept the re-proposal of the proposal that I proposed to him. It makes perfect sense to me. All set? Ready to go? Okay. I seek the wise and sage council of the boys at work.

(LIGHT change.)

EMILY. There is a place where philosophies are shaped, advice is given and decisions made. Happy hour!

(STEIN, HILL and McCARTHY stand drinking at a bar. EMILY joins them. Silence.)

WOOD PANELED TAP ROOMS

HILL. Mental illness.

EMILY. Too close to home.

STEIN. Marry the poor guy. Get it over with. *(All glare at him.)* Sorry. Lost my head.

MCCARTHY. Brown? One word. Frigid. *(All the men shudder.)* Men hate a frigid woman.

HILL. A frigid woman makes you blame yourself.

STEIN. A frigid woman makes you impotent *(They all stare at him.)* So I've heard.

MCCARTHY. No man wants a frigid woman. Be frigid.

EMILY. *(unconvinced)* It might work.

HILL. It works for my wife and me.

MCCARTHY. Okay, you and John are in bed together.

STEIN. John is reading. Get his attention.

HILL. John, being a very intelligent man, gets the picture. He puts his arms around you and begins kissing your neck. *(HILL chastely does so. EMILY squirms and giggles.)*

MCCARTHY. He wouldn't do it like that, Hill. Let me show you how'd he'd do it. *(McCARTHY chastely kisses EMILY'S neck. EMILY squirms and giggles.)*

HILL. Brown, you're responding.

EMILY. Guys, you're tickling. *(Pause. They ponder.)*

MCCARTHY. You are thinking of dead puppy dogs. *(EMILY gives a sympathetic little moan. McCARTHY kisses her neck. EMILY giggles.)* You're hopeless, Brown.

HILL. Wait! Me again! Of nuns. *(HILL kisses her neck. EMILY giggles.)*

HILL. Obviously Brown's not Catholic.

STEIN. Wait, wait, wait, wait. Let me show you how to kiss Brown's neck.

HILL. I haven't finished.

MCCARTHY. I want seconds.

STEIN. I haven't had firsts.

EMILY. Guys, you're not helping.

MCCARTHY. Brown, you're not concentrating!

HILL. We can only do so much, Brown.

STEIN. After all, this is a public place.

EMILY. I'll concentrate.

HILL. You are thinking of falling off a razorblade rusty ship in the middle of a raging, cold ocean and drowning. *(The boys murmur in approval. HILL kisses EMILY'S neck. EMILY squinches her face, trying not to giggle.)*

MCCARTHY. Brown. You are screaming for air, water stinging your eyes. *(A kiss. EMILY trembles.)*

HILL. Way to go, Brown.

STEIN. Waves. Waves buffeting you, waves dragging you down. *(A kiss. EMILY perseveres.)*

STEIN. Very nice.

HILL. Okay, Brown, here comes an all-out offensive.

MCCARTHY. Waves are rolling you over.

HILL. Good, Brown!

STEIN. Caressing your ears.

HILL. You can do it.

MCCARTHY. Your neck.

HILL. Your shoulders.

STEIN. Your arms. *(EMILY breaks into hysterical laughter. The boys cringe, embarrassed.)* Frigidity doesn't work.

HILL. Not when you're ticklish.

MCCARTHY. Ticklish women are responsive women. *(A

moment. They all look at EMILY with new respect.)
 EMILY. I'm not saying a word. *(They ponder.)*
 HILL. Let's go to the other extreme.
 STEIN. Good idea.
 EMILY. What?
 MCCARTHY. Perversion?
 HILL. Yes!
 STEIN. Of course.
 HILL. Perversion.

(The boys Exit. LIGHT change.)

 EMILY. *(puzzled)* Perversion?

TIMES SQUARE!

(LIGHTS up on EMILY and the boys. The boys are excited, wide eyed and rubber necking. STEIN now wears a cowboy hat, HILL, sunglasses and McCARTHY, a trenchcoat.)

 MCCARTHY. *(like a conductor)* Forty-Second Street, Triple X Time Square!
 EMILY. Guys—
 HILL. Girls, girls, girls!
 EMILY. Guys—
 STEIN. Porno-madness!
 EMILY. Guys! Where are you taking me?
 MCCARTHY. To an adult bookstore. Zip!
 HILL. Zoom!
 STEIN. Zowie! *(The men all Exit. Pause. The men all hurry back.)*

MCCARTHY. Brown, come on!

HILL. What's the matter?

STEIN. What's the problem?

HILL. Brown, this is not a neighborhood to stand on

EMILY. Look, I don't know about you guys but I get embarrassed even being with a man while he's buying *Playboy* magazine.

STEIN. Why?

EMILY. It makes me feel like I'm wearing a sign that says in big letters — yes, this is where my mind's at.

MCCARTHY. Isn't it?

HILL. You mean it's not?

MCCARTHY. I'm disappointed, Brown.

EMILY. Look, maybe it is but somehow I feel that other people aren't supposed to know that.

STEIN. Brown is having second thoughts.

HILL. Brown needs a disguise.

STEIN. Brown needs a cowboy hat. *(He takes off his hat and puts it on her head.)*

HILL. Brown needs some shades. *(He takes off his sunglasses and puts them on her.)*

MCCARTHY. Brown needs a trenchcoat. *(He takes off his trenchcoat and puts it on EMILY.)*

STEIN. Beautiful. Pull the collar up. Hunch over. Now shuffle when you walk.

EMILY. Am I recognizable?

HILL. Not as any woman I know. Let's go.

STEIN. Now, Brown, be prepared. We're talking dirt in this place.

MCCARTHY. We're talking smut and guilt.

HILL. We're talking marital aids! *(The boys hurry off.)*

EMILY. I just had the most awful feeling that someone was going to recognize me.

(HUGH BROWN Enters. He stops, shocked.)

HUGH. Emily!
EMILY. Daddy! *(Suddenly mortified, he shields his face and quickly Exits.)* Someone did.

(LIGHT change.)

EMILY. Okay! I bought a magazine. I took it home.

(LIGHTS up on a large double bed.)

EMILY. I called John at work and suggested he come over and spend the night.

(The SOUND of off-stage gargling.)

EMILY. Pretend for a moment, I'm wearing a nightgown. Covered with bunnies. I like bunnies. *(EMILY hurries to her briefcase. She opens it and takes out a magazine in a brown paper bag. Holding it extended like a dead skunk, EMILY hurries back to the bed. She puts the magazine beneath JOHN'S pillow. She leaps onto the bed.)* Sometimes I get such a kick out of myself.

(She rolls over and closes her eyes, feigning sleep. JOHN Enters. He pulls back the covers on his side of the bed. He fluffs his pillow and finds...)

JOHN. What's this?
EMILY. Mmm? Oh, no! Give me that! I thought I hid that! *(JOHN pulls the magazine out of the bag.)* John, don't! You don't want to look!
JOHN. Women who crave men? *(JOHN leafs coolly through the magazine.)*
EMILY. I'm so embarrassed, I ... you must think I'm a ... *(taking a quick glance)* Oh! Look at what they're — *(taking a close look)* Jesus, what *are* they doing? *(They huddle together, heads bent over the magazine.)*
JOHN. She's pretty limber.
EMILY. She sure is. And he must be strong.
JOHN. It's not strength ... *(turning the magazine)* ... it's balance. *(silence)* Wanna try?

(EMILY nods a wide eyed yes. JOHN moves to embrace her. LIGHTS to black. LIGHTS up on EMILY.)

EMILY. So we did. It was ... awesome! My life ... was a mess. It was time to face facts. It was time to take action. It was time to be cool, analytical and logical. It was time to throw myself off the Staten Island Ferry.

BATTERY PARK

(Enter HILL, STEIN, McCARTHY.)

HILL. Brown, we are talking viable alternatives.
MCCARTHY. We are talking divine intervention!
HILL. We are talking deus ex machina!

STEIN. Fields has thought of something!
MCCARTHY. Fields has!
EMILY. Fields?

(FIELDS is sitting on a parkbench, self importantly eating potato chips.)

HILL. Sit, Brown, sit!
FIELDS. You should have come to me immediately. You want info? Go to the expert.
MCCARTHY. Listen to this, Brown.
HILL. Fields is brilliant.
STEIN. Fields went to Harvard.
FIELDS. Infidelity. Set it up so it *looks* like you're having an affair, Brown. John will jump to conclusions. He'll be unreasonable. You can then be unreasonable back. He doesn't love you. He doesn't trust you. You hate it that he doesn't trust you.
MCCARTHY. *(with new respect)* How do you *know* all this, Fields?
FIELDS. Because I've never trusted women and they've always hated it! Marriage? No way! You're happy. He's happy. We're talking Pepsi generation.
HILL. Tell her, Fields.
FIELDS. We get together, you, me and John. I'll pay attention to you, Brown. A lot of attention. By the time I'm finished he'll have no choice but to believe you're having an affair with me.
MCCARTHY. It's perfect! Who would ever believe that Brown is having an affair with Fields?
EMILY. It's the stupidest idea I ever heard.

STEIN. Desperation calls for desperate measures.
EMILY. Am I that desperate? *(a thoughtful moment)*
THE BOYS. Yes.

(LIGHT change.)

EMILY. I took Fields with me to see some scenes in John's acting workshop. John was doing a scene from "A Streetcar Named Desire." John was playing—
FIELDS. *(as Marlon Brando)* Stella! *(FIELDS giggles happily.)*
EMILY. *(annoyed)* John was playing Stanley. Some... girl was playing Stella.
FIELDS. What a set of gunboats.
EMILY. Afterward everyone went to the local pub.

OLD CHELSEA BAR

(LIGHT change. A pub table. FIELDS and EMILY sit. FIELDS begins drinking beer and munching pretzels.)

FIELDS. Know what the scene was, Brown? It was organic. I know. I have organic tendencies. You could hardly tell they were acting.

(JOHN Enters and crosses to the table.)

JOHN. Be right with you. I'm just going over some notes with Bonnie.
EMILY. With who?
FIELDS. With Stella. Bark-bark-bark!

EMILY. Take your time. *(to herself: as he Exits)* Take all day.

FIELDS. They're gonna showcase it. I heard someone say. I bet the rehearsals will be very steamy stuff! Method acting, Brown! Sensitivity exercises! Torn t-shirts and everyone hating their mothers! Theatre is so great.

EMILY. *(staring)* She is all over him, Fields. She is entwined around him like a boa constrictor.

FIELDS. *(cupping his hands in front of his chest)* Homina-homina-homina.

EMILY. Jesus, doesn't she realize they're in a public place? *(waving; smiling cheerily)* Hi, Yes, I'm still here and I'm having a wonderful time. I wish I had a gun.

FIELDS. *(draining his beer)* Well ... all set? Ready to be swept off your feet? *(EMILY reaches out and grabs FIELDS in what is know in the vernacular as a "titty-twister." She twists.)*

EMILY. I'm going to kill you, Fields.

FIELDS. Ah! Brown, no, you don't understand, we're supposed to be romantically involved! *(EMILY twists.)*

FIELDS. Ah! Oh, I get it. S and M! Kinky, Brown, very kinky! *(EMILY twists.)*

FIELDS. Hah! Ah! Brown, please! We're supposed to be playing around behind his back!

EMILY. Not in a million billion years!

FIELDS. What?

EMILY. I don't want to give him ideas, you idiot! *(EMILY releases FIELDS and sadly stares.)*

FIELDS. Jesus, Brown, you really are screwed up.

EMILY. I used to be a happy woman, Fields. Now I'm miserable. I hate love.

ACT II   **EMILY**   71

FIELDS. Tell him the truth, Brown.
EMILY. I'll lose him if I tell him the truth.
FIELDS. Marry him.
EMILY. I'll lose him if I marry him.
FIELDS. Tell him the truth. You'll lose him sooner that way.

(LIGHT change.)

EMILY. The problem is we never know when we're well off, do we? The problem is that we always know when we're not. The problem is that we never know what we have until we don't have it anymore. Or is it that when we don't have it anymore, we make it better in our minds than it was to begin with? And so we wonder. And so we live our lives. We tell ourselves that we like being alone while in the same breath we admit that we hate being lonely. We fool ourselves by saying that when we meet the right person, we'll know it. And sometimes when we finally recognize the enemy, we realize the enemy is us. Lucky in life, unlucky in love. Laugh and get on with it. Isn't that how the story goes? *(a moment)* And outside it looks like rain.

(The sound of THUNDER rumbling. LIGHT change.)

RAINY CITY STREETS

(It's night. EMILY sits on a front stoop. JOHN Enters. He stops in surprise.)

JOHN. Well, hey, what are you doing here? Been waiting long?

EMILY. Yeah.

JOHN. You should have called.

EMILY. Called what, your service? Why don't you get a real phone? *(pause)* I want to talk. Can we sit?

JOHN. Let's go upstairs.

EMILY. Your roommates are there, right?

JOHN. Maybe.

EMILY. I can't deal with roommates.

JOHN. Okay, what's the matter?

EMILY. Please ... can we just sit?

JOHN. Okay. Talk to me.

EMILY. John ... Why do you want to marry me?

JOHN. You spring for cabs, you have a great apartment, what the hell.

EMILY. I'm serious.

JOHN. So am I.

EMILY. John!

JOHN. Emily. I love you.

EMILY. Okay. Tell me what that is. I bet you can't. I bet.

JOHN. Well, let's see. *(pause, looking at her)* Eyes.

EMILY. What about my eyes?

JOHN. Not yours, mine. *(a moment)* They can't look at you enough. *(a small smile, touching her ear)* Ears. The only thing mine want to hear ... is the sound of you. Even if it's just walking across a room. When my ears can hear you making any sound at all, I know you're close by. I don't know, I'm comforted by that. *(a moment)* The touch of you. I'm always wanting to touch you, Emily. When I pull you into bed and we're making love, sometimes it has nothing to do with passion. I just want to get as close as I can to you. Closer... than I can. *(a moment)* I've been waiting for you my whole life. Everything I've ever done and thought and felt, it was all just preparation for meeting you.

EMILY. *(moved almost to tears)* Oh, John, that was beautiful. *(forcing herself to snap out it)* But is that any reason to want to go and marry someone?

JOHN. Yes.

EMILY. *(without conviction)* You see, I am often of the opinion that love is not such a big deal. I mean, I bet I could stick you outside on a hot summer day when Columbus Avenue is an ocean of bouncing boobs in thin cotton tops and I bet you'd fall in love ten times in one block. Couldn't I do that? Uh-huh. I bet I could. So see, it's not a big deal.

JOHN. You're not talking about love.

EMILY. What am I talking about then?

JOHN. I don't know. You tell me.

EMILY. I'm talking about ... I'm talking about ... Oh! What I'm talking about is the fact that I can't marry you. Okay, go on, hate me, hit me, get it over with. I deserve it. I do nothing but mess people up and make people unhappy and—

JOHN. You know you don't do that.

EMILY. I do. I should go live in a leper colony. I should—

JOHN. Hey. Stop playing for my sympathy and tell me what's going on.

EMILY. What a mean, truthful thing to say. You always say such—

JOHN. Emily! Why can't you marry me?

(Silence. The rumble of THUNDER. The pitter-pat of RAIN, quickly growing into a rush.)

EMILY. I wasn't serious. When I asked you, I thought you'd say no. I never thought you'd ask me to marry you back. Why did you have to go and do such a dumb thing? Oh ... it wasn't a dumb thing. It was a wonderful thing. I'm a dumb thing. I ... I don't want to be married. *(silence)* We're going to catch pneumonia. *(silence)*
JOHN. You thought I'd say no.
EMILY. You hate me now.
JOHN. I'm just trying to understand.
EMILY. See, I thought I needed ... room.
JOHN. Room.
EMILY. To move.
JOHN. Where were you going to move, Emily?
EMILY. I ... don't know.
JOHN. Give me the ring, Emily.
EMILY. It's my ring.
JOHN. Give me the goddam ring. *(She takes it off and hands it to him. He looks at it a moment. He puts it into her hand and closes her hand around it.)* There. You save it for the next guy. *(He Exits without a word. She stands in silence.)*
EMILY. The rain pours down.

(LIGHT change.)

DROWNIN' YOUR SORROWS IN THE BLUES

(A bar. EMILY and HALLIE are at a table, drinking. They have been for quite awhile.)

EMILY. *(toasting)* To burnt bridges!
HALLIE. *(without enthusiasm)* Mmm.
EMILY. The hell with love, Hallie. I have a job, a career. My father is buying me a company to run into the ground for him. I'm supposed to give all that up to marry some man? No way.
HALLIE. Some people get married and continue to work, Emily.
EMILY. Hah! Some people? Men people. Women people get pregnant.
HALLIE. And take maternity leaves.
EMILY. Hallie, once you're out of the rotation, you never make it back into the starting line up. *(toasting)* To independence from egotistical, overly competitive, insensitive men!
HALLIE. *(a sigh)* Emily, sometimes I think we're not beatin' those men, we're joinin 'm. You can't fight nature, Emily. You can't fight the nesting instinct.
EMILY. Great. First we're women, now we're ducks.
HALLIE. Me, me, me. It's all we think about. We all have to have the best marks, go to the best schools, get the most blue ribbons. We're all so damn busy provin' how wonderful we are, we don't leave ourselves time to think or doubt.
EMILY. You have to prove yourself if you want any kind of a career.
HALLIE. Emily, don't get mad but ... know what a career is? It's some dumb, fancy name for havin' to work for

a living. And where this idea that workin' for a living is fun came from, I'll never know. The hell with it! *(A moment. EMILY takes something from her purse.)*

EMILY. Look at this.

HALLIE. What is it.

EMILY. A flyer. It was taped in the window of the restaurant.

HALLIE. Oooh! "A Streetcar Named Desire."

EMILY. It's an Off-off-off-off-off-off Broadway showcase production. John's in it. With Bonnie.

HALLIE. Who's Bonnie? *(EMILY cups her hands in front of her breats.)*

EMILY. Homina-homina-homina.

HALLIE. Tonight. You gotta go!

EMILY. Absolutely not. I don't want him back.

HALLIE. You don't want him back?

EMILY. I don't want him back.

HALLIE. You sure you don't want him back?

EMILY. Maybe I want him back. *(a moment)* Hallie, help me.

HALLIE. You've got to get his attention.

EMILY. How?

HALLIE. Feminine wiles.

EMILY. To feminine wiles! What do I do once I've gotten his attention with my feminine wiles?

HALLIE. You do what women have done since the beginning of time. Break into hysterical tears and cry till he begs you to stop. *(They laugh. And then suddenly, they begin to cry. They sob, their hearts broken. Suddenly they laugh again.)*

EMILY. What a ya think?

HALLIE. S'wonderful.

(A WAITER approaches with another round of drinks.)

EMILY. M' having man trouble.
WAITER. *(very straight)* Join the club, sweets. *(Exits)*
HALLIE. To feminine wiles? *(They toast.)*
HALLIE and EMILY. To feminine wiles!

(LIGHT change. LIGHTS to HALLIE.)

HALLIE. Hi. Surprise. It's me, Hallie. Well, we got so drunk that night. And what happened is not Emily's fault. I encouraged her. We decided she should go see John in his play. It would be a nice gesture. And then, she could go backstage after, and wouldn't he be happy to see her — a' course he would! — and a' course just to be polite he'd take her out for a burger and a beer or two or three and then — boom! — home to bed and everything would be fine at least until the next morning when he might be angry again but then Emily could make him feel guilty cause he'd slept with her. This is feminine wiles! This did not work. What happened was ... well, you'll see. I just love "A Streetcar Named Desire."

THE KINDNESS OF STRANGERS!

(From the back of the house, EMILY Enters into the audience. She is quite drunk but is trying not to show it. She is followed by a helpless house manager. LIGHTS up on stage. The play is going, full bore, yet it is somewhat disjointed as if seen through the eyes of a drunken EMILY.)

USHER. Stop. Miss! You can't go in. There's a performance in progress. Miss! There's a performance!
EMILY. That is why ... I'm here.
USHER. You can't go in now.
EMILY. I am the critic for the *Times.*
HALLIE/STELLA. Drunk, drunk, animal thing, you!
EMILY. What!?
USHER. Sssssshhhhh!
EMILY. Sssssshhhhh!
DEIRDRE/BLANCHE. My sister is going to have a baby!
EMILY. A baby!?
MCCARTHY/MITCH. This is terrible.
EMILY. This's terrible.
USHER. Miss!
EMILY. Sssssshhhhh! *(EMILY moves across a row, almost falling into people's laps. The USHER follows.)* Ssssshhhh!
USHER. Sit down.
EMILY. Don't tell me to sit down. I'm from the *Times.*
USHER. Sssssssshhhhhh!
EMILY. Sssssssssssssssssshhhhhhhhhhhhhhh!
DEIRDRE/BLANCHE. Lunacy, absolute lunacy.
EMILY. This's ... absolute lunacy.
MCCARTHY/MITCH. Will you shut up! *(EMILY giggles.)*
USHER. Miss, there's a seat there.
EMILY. Thank you.
USHER. You're on his foot!
EMILY. I'm terribly sorry.
USHER. Get off of it.
EMILY. I'm terribly sorry.
FIELDS/PABLO. I think coffee would do him a world of good.

EMILY. I think coffee would do *me* a world of good.
USHER. Really!
EMILY. It's all right. Really. I'm from the *Times*. *(EMILY sits.)*
FIELDS/PABLO. Let's get out of here.
MCCARTHY/MITCH. Poker should not be played in a house with women!
USHER. Now control yourself.
EMILY. Thank you. *(She waves back down the row.)* I've always depended on the kindness of strangers!

(She giggles like that's the funniest thing she's ever heard. A roar on stage. JOHN/STANLEY Enters with telephone.)

JOHN/STANLEY. My baby doll's left me.
EMILY. Oh!
JOHN/STANLEY. Eunice? I want my baby!!
EMILY. I'm your baby!
JOHN/STANLEY. Eunice! I'll keep ringing till I talk to my baby! Stella! Stella, sweetheart!
EMILY. Oh! I'm your sweetheart!
JOHN/STANLEY. Stella!
EMILY. *(Calls toward the stage.)* John!
JOHN/STANLEY. Stella! I want my baby down here!
EMILY. I want my baby down here!
JOHN. Stellaaaaaaaaaa! *(EMILY leaps to her feet and unleashes a skyshattering bellow.)*
EMILY. Johnnnnnnnnnnnnnnnnnnnnnnn! *(JOHN gets off his knees and rushes to the edge of the stage.)*
JOHN. What! Is your problem, Emily?
EMILY. I ... I want you to come with me. *(JOHN furiously*

stares at her a long moment. And then he turns and walks off stage. Silence. EMILY walks out of the audience and up onto the stage. She lies down, using her briefcase as a pillow.) Pretty bad, huh? Pretty horrible thing to do? Unforgivable? You better believe it. There are mornings in your life when consciousness sneaks up on you like a gang tackle. The waves of guilt are so overpowering you want your whole life to just go away. But it won't.

(A PHONE rings and then a voice echos throughout the theatre.)

> VOICE. Columbus Central.
> EMILY. Is John Stone working?
> VOICE. He quit.
> EMILY. When?
> VOICE. This afternoon.
> EMILY. Did he leave a number?
> VOICE. No. He has a service.
> EMILY. He's terminated service. Did he leave an address?
> VOICE. Yeah. Minnesota.
> EMILY. Are you sure?
> VOICE. Honey, he didn't even hang around to work happy hour. Sorry.

(The SOUND of a hang-up.)

> EMILY. *(to the audience:)* Love ... is never having to say you're sorry. Right. Sometimes sorry is all you get.

(LIGHT change.)

CARAMBA!

(The SOUNDS of a crowded bar, of milling noisy people, of a Mexican band. FIELDS, HILL, McCARTHY and STEIN Enter singing and talking. They carry glasses and pitchers of margaritas.)

STEIN. There she is!
HILL. 'Bout time!
MCCARTHY. Join us for a margarita, Brown!
HILL. They're running a special.
FIELDS. Drink up! We all will!
STEIN. We were just talking about you.
MCCARTHY. Damn right.
FIELDS. We love ya, Brown, we love ya!
HILL. Query. Whatever happened to happy ever after?
STEIN. Whatever happened to death do us part?
MCCARTHY. Where has love gone, Brown?
FIELDS. Onto the trash heap.
HILL. Into the toilet.
STEIN. Down the drain.
MCCARTHY. You wanna know who we blame?
THE BOYS. You!
EMILY. Would someone please order me a large glass of grain alcohol?
MCCARTHY. Not just you, Brown, but women in general. You don't take a good man for granted.
FIELDS. Romeo, Romeo, wherefore art thou, Romeo?
STEIN. Working.

HILL. Scared of dying.
MCCARTHY. Where the hell are *you?*
EMILY. I'm really not in the mood for this.
STEIN. Brown, we've been talking.
HILL. It is our feeling you owe John an apology.
(EMILY stifles a groan.)
STEIN. Apologizing is a wonderful institution.
MCCARTHY. If your apology is accepted you're off the hook.
STEIN. And if it's not, your guilt is transferred to the dolt who doesn't have the compassion and good sense to understand that even the best and brightest of us make mistakes.
FIELDS. Apologize, Brown! Drink up. Let me refill your glass.
EMILY. Attention, boys, attention! You can't apologize if there's no one to apologize to.
MCCARTHY. What do you mean?
EMILY. John moved back to Minnesota. *(pause)*
HILL. Sorry, Brown.
STEIN. Too bad, kid.
EMILY. I had an apology. A well constructed combination of logic and groveling. I deserved a chance to give it. I mean, I'm not a bad person if you can overlook my insecurity, my immaturity and my deceitfulness for which there is a good is not altogether believable explanation.
HILL. Have a margarita.
FIELDS. We all will.
EMILY. Oh, god ... I want to start over. I want to pretend that what happened, never happened. I want to get it in gear. It's time to return to normal! Guys? Give me that margarita!

FIELDS. Let's all have one! *(The boys all cheer.)*
HILL. Brown! Let me tell you something. He didn't take you back because he's an egotistical child whose pride was hurt.
STEIN. And so what if he didn't? Not to worry. Boys like you, Brown.
MCCARTHY. Brown? Never beg.
FIELDS. Unless you have no other choice.
THE BOYS. Exactly.
STEIN. And Brown, we'll say this and then we'll shut up.
FIELDS. Make this the last time you put out for any bozo who waits tables.
THE BOYS. Exactly!
MCCARTHY. Not a word. We're always glad to help.
EMILY. Guys!? Dinner's on me!

(CHEERS and CHATTER. A toast. LIGHT change.)

EMILY. Days follow days. Work. Oh, sweet work. No time to be alone. No time to think. Anything to keep from hearing a certain voice in your head. Eighteen-hour days. Sweat it all out at the health club. After working out, descend on the finest and newest restaurants like packs of finely attired wolves, ravenous for good times. And then dancing. Skip the light fantastic. Parties. People. Sophisticated conversation. Champagne. Cocaine. Music and laughter. What's love got to do with it? What is love but a second-hand emotion? God help me, Hallie's right. We don't leave ourselves time to think or doubt.

THE NEW YORK CITY SKYLINE AT NIGHT

(DEIRDRE Enters carrying a glass of champagne.)

EMILY. It's a beautiful view.

DEIRDRE. Yes. Many's the night I've sat alone in this lovely apartment contemplating the shards of my wasted life and time after time — it never fails, really — I'm comforted by the knowledge that I have a beautiful view.

EMILY. Mother, please, not tonight.

DEIRDRE. I see. *(They silently contemplate the view.)*

EMILY. I'm going to cry.

DEIRDRE. Oh, really, Emily.

EMILY. I don't know if I'm coming or going.

DEIRDRE. That's because you won't have a glass of champagne.

EMILY. Mother! Why am I always unhappy!?

DEIRDRE. You're happy, darling. You're like me, though. You're not satisfied. I think that's healthy. It keeps one from becoming complacent.

EMILY. You're impossible. I can never tell when you're being serious and when you're not.

DEIRDRE. I'm *always* serious, darling, even *when* I'm not. *(pause)*

EMILY. Mother? Did you and Daddy every really care about one another?

DEIRDRE. Oh, Emily, is that what this is all about?

EMILY. Answer me, Mother, just this once.

DEIRDRE. Of course we did, darling. Don't you know your father fell in love with me at first sight?

EMILY. You're kidding.

DEIRDRE. Hardly. He did. And I suppose in my own way, yes, I was in love with him.

EMILY. But you left him. *(pause)*

DEIRDRE. I graduated from Smith College eighth in a class of brilliant, brilliant women to enter a world that expected nothing more of me than marriage to a man like your father. I was to be seen, smiling always, but seldom heard. An over-qualified brood mare. It made me angry, darling. I am angry. And I was right. I see friends who hung on, who raised the children, who gave the dinner parties, who cleaned up the dog shit, dumped. Divorced. Left for smoother skin and higher bosoms. Left with large, empty houses and a membership at the club and time on their hands. *That,* my darling, is unhappiness. So I'll be dissatisfied, thank you. And I'll count my blessings. And you should too. You and I, Emily, answer to no one but ourselves.

EMILY. You're right. In your own way, you always are. But I still want to know something. I want to know one darn thing.

DEIRDRE. What's that?

EMILY. Who *do* you turn to when you're old? *(She leaves.)*

DEIRDRE. *(staring at the view)* Call me, darling.

(LIGHT change.)

THE NEW YORK STOCK EXCHANGE

(HUGH and EMILY Enter.)

HUGH. Now they're going to be particularly concerned with your position for foreign markets, I — Emily, you're not paying attention.

EMILY. Sorry, Daddy.

HUGH. Emily, your behavior of the past few weeks is completely unacceptable. I've been watching. I'm not going to stand for it any longer. There is too much at stake here, my dear.

EMILY. It's just a company, Daddy.

HUGH. And I want it! I want you to run it! Two hours from now, we meet with their board of directors. I won't mince words. It's an inspection. You are exhibit A. I want you to show them, to show me, that you're capable of doing the job I know you can do. I want you to blow their boats out of the water, Emily. The pressure is on. Time to get your priorities straight. Now! As I was saying. Foreign markets—

EMILY. Daddy, did you love Mother?

HUGH. Emily, will you concentrate on the business at hand?

EMILY. She says you fell in love with her at first sight.

HUGH. Good god! Of all the — she said that?

EMILY. Did you? *(Silence. HUGH nods.)*

HUGH. *(softly)* She never believed me. When you don't like yourself much, it's hard to believe anyone else can. *(silence)*

EMILY. Do you regret it? Meeting her. Marrying her.

HUGH. Good god. If I hadn't had her, I wouldn't have you. *(pause)* May we do some work now, please? One can love or one can work, one cannot do both. Foreign markets!

EMILY. Daddy, I don't think I'm the right person for this job.

HUGH. Nonsense.

EMILY. I think you should consider someone else.

HUGH. Perhaps *you'd* like to consider looking for a position elsewhere. *(pause)*

EMILY. I just considered.

HUGH. What?

EMILY. I quit.

HUGH. What!? Don't be ridiculous. What are you doing? Where are you going?

EMILY. *(Exiting)* Minnesota

HUGH. Emily! You're being hasty. You're making an emotional decision and you're not thinking clearly. Dammit, Emily, what about my company!?

EMILY. You'll have to run it yourself.

HUGH. *(Exiting)* Emily! Emily!

(LIGHT change.)

A HOME IN THE PINE TREES

(EMILY Enters.)

EMILY. Minnesota! Home of the Golden Gophers. Nordic types in flannel shirts and down vests. The Minnesota Vikings. It was November and so to be safe I rented a Ford Bronco with four wheel drive, studded tires and a snowmobile in the back. I headed north. Through woods. Past lakes that glittered in the sunshine. When you live in Manhattan you forget that the sky is so big. John's family had a beautiful house. I knew they'd all be happy that I'd come. It was the day before Thanksgiving and I arrived bearing gifts. I brought cold cuts from Zabars.

(LIGHT change. JOHN is sitting on a couch. He has a shotgun in his lap that he cleans. EMILY joins him.)

EMILY. Your parents have a beautiful home.

(Pause. The sound of a DOG BARKING.)

EMILY. You have a very large dog. I think he's attracted to my Ford Bronco. *(pause)* So you're back for good.
JOHN. Here?
EMILY. Yes.
JOHN. Actually I'm thinking of giving L.A. a shot. I thought I'd get some sunglasses and gold chains, drive a sportscar, find some nineteen-year-old blonde hardbody to play with.
EMILY. Are you implying my body's not hard?
JOHN. Your body's fine.
EMILY. Then would you please make love to me right here and now on this couch?
JOHN. Emily, my parents sit on this couch.
EMILY. It would do a lot to convince me that you don't hate me.
JOHN. I don't know how I feel about you.
EMILY. A mixed up girl hurts your feelings and you decide to drive sportscars.

JOHN. Jesus, Emily. Look, I'm not going to Los Angeles. And no, I'm not back here for good. I ... I never planned to be. I'm just home for the holidays.
EMILY. You didn't come home because of me?
JOHN. No.
EMILY. I told people I'd driven you away.
JOHN. I'm sure.
EMILY. They were very impressed.
JOHN. After New Year's, I'm back in New York.
EMILY. Couldn't you at least wait until Easter?
JOHN. There are several influential people who saw my work and when they were allowed to sit through it actually enjoyed it. You haven't driven me out of New York.
EMILY. I'm glad.
JOHN. Don't always give yourself so much credit.
EMILY. Don't be so mean.
JOHN. I'll be any way I want. *(He cleans his shotgun. Silence.)*
EMILY. My, what big guns you have.
JOHN. Better to shoot things with.
EMILY. Ohhh.
JOHN. You ever hunt, Emily, a "liberated" modern woman like you?
EMILY. You mean, like ... Bambi?
JOHN. Deer. Bear. Birds. A *man* is a hunter, Emily. A man's job is to put food on the table. A man's job is to know his prey. He knows its habits, its secrets, its innermost thoughts. What do you think of that?
EMILY. I don't think I could ever eat anything I was so intimately involved with. What's a woman's job, Mr.

Suddenly-Madly-Macho? Cooking what the caveman brings home? Well, I don't cook.

JOHN. How do you eat?

EMILY. You know how I eat. Out.

JOHN. There's a Thanksgiving tradition in this house, for family and guests alike. Some of us cook up the feast. Some of us play football in the backyard. Who are you with?

EMILY. *(asserting herself)* I'm with the men.

(LIGHT change.)

TURKEYS

EMILY. Picture it. Six feet of golden tanned skin and blonde hair takes a lateral out of mid air and sweeps right, running with grace and abandon. Now into your field of vision run two other awesomely athletic types. You are picturing what is referred to as a perfect Green Bay Sweep. Defenders run to intercept. Bodies collide and tumble. The runner is dragged to the ground. The girls all slap high fives. And me? I'm in the kitchen with the men putting together goddam Thanksgiving dinner.

(JOHN comes up behind EMILY and ties an apron around her waist.)

JOHN. Come on, Emily, let's go! Times a wastin'. *(They move to a large butcher block table.)*

EMILY. What do I do? *(JOHN hands EMILY a large turnip and a knife.)*

JOHN. Cut that up.
EMILY. What is it, an armadillo?
JOHN. A turnip. Cube it. *(He Exits.)*
EMILY. *(to the audience:)* Outside in the backyard, the beautiful norse goddesses were throwing each other long perfect touchdown passes. Inside the men cooked and chopped and simmered and basted and powdered with flour and seasoned and set the table. Pies and cookies came out of the oven. The turkey turned brown. The stupid-ass ham got glazed. Through all this, I attack the turnip with my knife. It won't cooperate. It rolls off the cutting board. It won't cut no matter how hard I hack and heave. When I get the knife into it, I can't get it out. I am perspiring. I am pissed off. *(whispering at the turnip)* Gimme a break. Let me look good just once. I'll make this as painless as possible, promise. Ready? All set? Okay. You're history.

(The knife comes down. LIGHTS to black. The sound of EMILY crying out in pain.)

EMILY. Oh! oh-oh-oh-oh-oh-oh ... is there a doctor in the house?

(LIGHTS up on JOHN putting the finishing touches on a beautifully set dining room table. EMILY, with a huge bandage on her thumb, glumly Enters. Silence.)

EMILY. Have I ruined everyone's appetite?
JOHN. I don't think so.
EMILY. The knife just ... slipped.

JOHN. You may never professionally cook again. *(Awkward silence. She begins folding napkins.)*

EMILY. It's a big table.

JOHN. It's a big family. *(pause)* Everybody introducing themselves?

EMILY. Everybody is being wonderful.

JOHN. *(pause)* Everybody thinks you're a nice person.

EMILY. Mmm, story of my life. Everybody? *(silence)*

JOHN. I like holidays. People come home.

EMILY. I'm not real big on holidays.

JOHN. No? Why not?

EMILY. Well ... I visit friends. We go out for drinks. Maybe I join someone for dinner. It's just another day off, really. Sometimes I just stay in bed.

JOHN. I think that's sad.

EMILY. I think it all depends on what you have to compare it to. *(A moment. JOHN starts to Exit. He suddenly stops. He turns and stares at her.)* **What?** *(He moves to her, gently raises her chin and kisses her.)*

JOHN. I'm very glad you're here for Thanksgiving.

(He Exits. LIGHT change.)

EMILY. Imagine if you will, people sitting around this Thanksgiving table. Imagine it laden with splendid-looking food. Imagine tableware glimmering in candlelight. Heads are bowed in a moment of silent grace. All have joined hands; grown-ups, the children. Imagine if you can what it's like to be suddenly overwhelmed by a sense of *family.* John and I are across from each other.

Here and here. We look up, catch the other's eyes. He seems to kiss me without touching. And suddenly ... I realize that tears are running down my cheeks. Stupid. I wipe them away. Stupid. I rise from the table. Excuse me for a moment? I walk quickly from the room. I don't look back. *(She moves from the table.)* Oh ... I can't stand feeling like this. What am I doing here? This is not me. This is not what I'm about. What in god's name am I doing here?

(LIGHT change. EMILY walks to the side of the stage and picks up a suitcase. She moves back center as JOHN Enters.)

MINNESOTA MOON

JOHN. Emily? *(realizing)* You're leaving.
EMILY. *(cheerfully)* Thought I would.
JOHN. You weren't going to tell me?
EMILY. Come on, you should be with someone else.
JOHN. I never asked "someone else" to marry me.
EMILY. Maybe someone else should have asked you first. *(He stares st her.)* Sorry. Bad joke. *(silence)*
JOHN. Where do we start, Emily? How do we even begin?
EMILY. We don't. It would never work. We're too different. I'm doing this for you, really. I care about you enough to end this now. *(silence)*
JOHN. What a crock of shit. You're doing this for me? Don't. I can take care of myself. This is about you.
EMILY. Me?
JOHN. Yeah, you. You don't know who you are. You

don't know what you want. You are so afraid.

EMILY. You and your expectations. You're always getting dissapointed. Well, I never do.

JOHN. Oh, no. You're happy as a clam, especially on holidays when you can sit around an empty room by yourself. *(pause)* You think you're the only one with doubts? People have doubts. When I asked you to marry me I wasn't saying I was going to love you the rest of my life. I was saying that I choose to try. Two big words. Choose. Try. Maybe we fail. The way things are these days, yeah, okay, probably we fail. But that's okay. What else is there? Tell me. I need to know what else there is.

EMILY. I...

JOHN. What?

EMILY. I just ... I don't know ...

JOHN. Will you talk!?

EMILY. I mean, I'm going along and I'm — you know — but then I can't help it, I...

JOHN. Spit it out!

EMILY. I want to be alone! I don't choose to try! I like being alone! Feeling like this doesn't happen when I'm alone! *(Silence. He just stares at her.)* I hate it when feelings get hurt. I just, see, I can't, I'm not a ... just everything.

JOHN. Get out of here.

EMILY. John, I want you to know ... I hope we can remain friends.

JOHN. Will you leave? *(She turns to leave. At the last moment:)* Emily. *(pause)* Travel safe.

(He Exits. LIGHT change.)

EMILY. I did. How do I love thee? Let me count the ways. There's a poem that starts that way. Like traditional wedding vows, it's out of date and needs to be rewritten. How do I love thee? Let me count the ways. I love thee like a beautiful place but you should know that I'm restless and I've never had a home. I love thee like the morning and the evening and the time between but you should know I'm afraid of growing old and the passing days drive me crazy. I love thee like in the movies but tell me what do we do when happy ever after fades to day after day and suddenly the credits roll? I am afraid I'll be hurt. I am afraid I'll hurt you. I am afraid to take chances. I would love you more but I have never learned to love me. Life is pleasant enough without commitments. I wish I could have told you that. *(a moment)* So. Let me tell you about me these days.

THE NEW YORKER'S MAP OF AMERICA

EMILY. I wake up in the morning. I wake up when I wake up, not before. I like to lie in bed and stare at the prints on the bedroom wall. I have one of those maps of the United States that shows all the avenues, the Hudson River and then Los Angeles. I stuck a little gold star in where Minnesota would be. The phone will ring. It's Daddy. He wants to know when I'm coming back to work. I tell him I don't know. I don't know when I'll know. The phone will ring and it's Hallie. She wants to know when I'm going to start dating again. She thinks it's unhealthy to spend so much time alone. I tell her I'm tired of trying to like people. The phone will ring and it's Deirdre. She's decided she wants to be a grandmother. All her friends are and she wants to be too. Give me time, Mom. The phone will ring and it's ... a wrong number.

THE NEW YORK SKYLINE

EMILY. I go running. I'm up to four miles a day. this time of year, the grounds of the park are covered with snow but the drive is cleared and I run on the pavement. I run easily. My stride is long and steady and my breath turns to steam in the cold air. Sometimes I stop and stare at the tops of the buildings that surround the park. They look like kings and queens and bishops and knights on a chess board. I don't have to tell you who the pawns are. Sometimes I stop and stare at ... nothing. I wonder if I made a mistake. I wonder if I've run out of second chances. I wonder if ever again a man will ask me out for something as innocent as a milkshake.

(She gives us a small, undefeated smile. LIGHTS fade to black on EMILY.)

END OF PLAY

PROP LIST

SR PRESET
Champagne bottle
Towel & evian
Slide clicker
Ribbon bouquet
3 shower presents
Grocery bag
Bud vase
Flower vase
Box matches
Ash tray
2 tavern men.
Paper towels
1 basket pretzels
Flashlight
5 sandwiches
5 napkins
Cocktail napkins
Plate
Soup bowl
White tablecloth
Grey tablecloth
Cheese doodles
3 waiter pads
Mop
Pens/pencils

E. briefcase
- Lipstick
- Compact
- $20 bills
- Bentwood

COCKTAILS

ACT I
- 2 wine/E & J
- 1 wine/E
- 3 cafe/R
  - Coke, wine, beer
- 3 party/champagne, martini, beer
- 3 Fields martini
- 2 water pitchers

ACT II
- 2 martini/E & H
- 1 champagne/D
- Scotch, beer, martini
- 5 margarita
- 2 margarita pitchers

SL PRESET
40's phone
H/portfolio
2 Coke cans/DL
E/suitcase
1 turnip/paring knife
1 basket pretzels
Arrow head
X word puzzle & pen

EMILY

2 white towels
S.C. flyer
Ashtray
Hotdogs
Thumb/DL
Gun, case, rag
COCKTAILS
ACT I
    Bloody Mary
    4 party/2 beer, martini, gin
    1 Fields martini
    2 water glasses
ACT II
    2 beers
    2 martini

SR FURNITURE
Bar stool
Eleg. table 2 chairs
2 cafe chairs
Bench
3 bentwood
X-bike
T.G.T.
Stoop

SL FURNITURE
Hotdog cart: buns
Couch
Butcher block:
   knife, turnip

3 cafe tables
4 cafe chairs
2 bentwood
H/desk
Pub table
Chelsea table

BED
Sheets
2 pillows
Candle
Wooden matches
Jar

ACT II
Strike matches
Add comforter & mag.

DRESSING ROOMS
E/X pen: breast pocket
Ring & box out L pkt.

MEN
4 wallets & $
$ clip—James

COSTUMES

EMILY
I-1
Blouse
Necklace
Ring
Watch
Skirt (suit)
Pantyhose
Shoes
Earrings
On back of chair:
   Jacket w/pocket scarf

I-2
Add: ribbon tie
   put on jacket

I-3 to II-3
Same

II-4
Teddy

II-5 to II-14
Same as I-2

II-15
Add: plaid vest

II-16
Same & apron (black & white)

II-17 to II-20
Same

JON STONE
I-7
Black pants
White shirt
Black tie
Black socks
Black shoes
2 aprons

I-10
T-shirt
Nylon shorts
Socks
Running shoes

I-12
Guthrie T-shirt
Work shirtBlue jeans
Belt
Socks
Shoes

I-13 & I-14
Same

I-16
Tweed jacket
Sweater vest
Slacks
Shirt
Tie
Socks
Shoes

I-17 to I-21
Same

I-24
Waiter costume

II-4
Briefs

II-10
"Stanley outfit"
T-shirt
Overshirt
Pants
Belt
Socks
Shoes

II-15
Black & white football jersey
Plaid flannel shirt
Blue jeans
Socks
Shoes

II-16
Add: apron w/bib (black & white)

II-18
Same w/out apron

HUGH BROWN
I-3
As waiter

I-4
Black suit
White shirt
Green tie
Black belt
Black socks
Black shoes

I-11
Same

I-13
Hot dog vendor

I-22
Same as I-4

I-24
Waiter costume

II-3
Same as I-4
Add:
   Trenchcoat
Cowboy hat
Sunglasses

II-12
Same as I-4

II-13
Hosp. gown

HALLIE
I-6
Grey sweat pants
Grey short sleeve T-shirt
Purple over shirt
Yellow socks
Yellow shoes

I-15
Black trendy dress
Black stockings

Black shoes
Pink glasses

I-18
Dress
Scarf

I-24
Patron
No change

II-1
Black dress w/jacket

II-9
Wide leg pants
Black loose top
Neck scarf
Black shoes
Jewelry

II-10
As Stella
House coat

DEIRDRE
I-15
Black & white suit
  Jacket
  Skirt
  Blouse

Pantyhose
Shoes
Purse
Jewelry

I-18
Same w/out jacket

I-24
Patron
No change

II-8
Black & white suit #2
Blouse
Burgundy accesories

II-10
As House Mgr.
Black smock

MC CARTHY
I-1
As Sean
Shirt
Pants

I-3
Suit
Shirt

Tie
Suspenders/belt
Socks
Shoes

I-5
Jogger

I-7
Patron
No change

I-11
Same as I-3

I-15
Woman

I-17
Same as I-3

I-24
Patron
No change

II-2
Same

II-3
Same
Add trenchcoat

II-5
Same

II-9
As waiter

II-10
As Mitch

II-11
Same as I-3

II-13
Same

STEIN
I-1
As Jason

I-3
Suit
Shirt
Tie
Suspenders/belt
Socks
Shoes

I-5
Jogger

I-7
Patron
No change

I-11
Same as I-3

I-15
Woman

I-18
Same as I-3

I-22
As Mr. Robinson
Add hat
Carry coat

I-24
Patron
No change

II-2
Same

II-3
Same
Add cowboy hat

II-5
Same

II-11 to II-13
Same

HILL
I-3
Suit
Shirt
Tie
Suspenders/belt
Socks
Shoes

I-5
Jogger

I-7
Waiter

I-9
Waiter

I-11
Same as I-3

I-15
Woman

I-18
Same as I-3

I-24
Waiter

II-2
Same as I-3

II-3
Same
Add sunglasses

II-5
Same

II-11 to II-13
Same

FIELDS
I-1
As waiter

I-3
Suit
Shirt
Tie
Suspenders/belt
Socks
Shoes

I-5
Jogger